Damming the Danube

Damming the Danube

Gabčikovo and Post-Communist Politics in Europe

John Fitzmaurice

WestviewPress

A Division of HarperCollins*Publishers*

For G.P.

Copyright © 1996 by Westview Press, A Division of HarperCollins Publishers, Inc.

Published in 1996 in the United States of America by Westview Press, 5500 Central Avenue, Boulder, Colorado 80301-2877, and in the United Kingdom by Westview Press, 12 Hid's Copse Road, Cumnor Hill, Oxford OX2 9JJ

Library of Congress Cataloging-in-Publication Data
Fitzmaurice, John.
  Damming the Danube: Gabčikovo and post-communist politics in Europe / by John Fitzmaurice.
    p. cm.
  Includes bibliographical references and index.
  ISBN 0-8133-2164-6 (hard)
  1. Water resources development—Political aspects—Danube River
Region. 2. Water resources development—Social aspects—Danube
River Region. 3. Hungary—Foreign relations—Slovakia.
4. Slovakia—Foreign relations—Hungary. 5. Political stability—Danube
River Region. 6. Europe—Politics and government—1989–
7. Gabčikovo (Power Plant) I. Title.
HD1697.5.D358F57   1996
333.91'009496—dc20   96-11288
                                                                            CIP

The paper used in this publication meets the requirements of the American National Standard for Permanence of Paper for Printed Library Materials Z39.48-1984.

10   9   8   7   6   5   4   3   2   1

Contents

Acknowledgments

I owe a debt of gratitude to the very many people who helped me freely and with great enthusiasm on this project. First, I must mention President Arpâd Gönsz, President of Hungary, who did me the honour of receiving me and expressing his support for the project. I should also like to thank State Secretary Tatar, Members of Parliament from all the major Hungarian political parties, Mr. Janos Vargha of the Danube Circle, Professors Valki and Nagy of the ELTE University and Hungarian legal team for giving me their time and expertise.

In Slovakia, I owe a particular debt to then Foreign Minister Kučan and former Minister Hofbauer, Deputy Speaker Prokès, Dr. Binder, Director of Vodohospodarska Vystaba and Mr. Liška, also of Vodohospodariska Vystaba, who took me to visit the site and initiated me into its complexities. Nor should I forget Mr. Vrsansky, Head of the Legal Department of the Foreign Office, now representing Slovakia in the Hague or Mr. Ambassador Chmel, Czechoslovak Ambassador in Budapest until April 1, 1993. I must mention Mr. Hrasko, Minister of the Environment in the Moravčik government.

In Vienna, Mrs. Radzyner of ORF, Mr. Fušak of the APA agency and Mr. Meister of the Bundes Umweltamt were guides to the "Austrian Connection" angle.

My thanks are also due to Mr. Michael Leigh of the EC Commission in Brussels.

Very special thanks are due to Tamas Kende of the International Law Department of the ELTE University in Budapest for so expertly organising my meetings in Hungary. Without his help, this book would not have been possible. I should also like to thank Mrs. Kovačova of the Press Department of the Slovak Foreign Ministry for skilfully arranging meetings in Bratislava.

Once again, Ms. Anna Isaac has expertly transformed my hieroglyphics into a tidy manuscript, coping with many difficult words in Slovak and

Hungarian with patience and professionalism. Nor would I wish to forget Susan McEachern, Senior Editor of Westview for her enthusiastic support for this project and her hard work in bringing it to fruition.

Last, let me state clearly that responsibility for any errors are mine, as are the views expressed and conclusions reached, though I have tried to let all the various contending views on this controversial issue find fair expression. This is more than the usual disclaimer on an issue which is such a political, scientific and legal minefield.

John Fitzmaurice

Preface

The Nagymaros-Gabčikovo project for a dam on the Danube River on the Hungarian Slovak border is a powerful and potentially explosive symbol, but a symbol with many readings.

For those who promoted the project, essentially the former communist régimes in Czechoslovakia and Hungary and parts of the Austrian banking and energy utility establishment, it was a symbol of progress, economic independence, control over nature, national pride and prestige. For its opponents, Greens and central European dissidents, it was a symbol of everything that was wrong with the communist system in Central Europe: a prestige project that would violate the Danube River, destroy the environment and traditional ways of life; a project that no longer had--if it ever did--an adequate economic justification to counterbalance the environmental damage. Politically, it was an example of the stubborn conservatism and stagnation of old style communist leaders and their refusal to adapt and respond to increasingly critical voices in society. It was, too, an example of the paradoxical collusion of Conservative Communists and western financial interests so characteristic of the 1970s and 1980s. It was a collusion that sought to defend the status quo, east and west.

The aim of this book will be to explore the complex ramifications of this massive project. We shall seek to explore and understand how the project came into being. We shall look at its purpose, its intended economic advantages. We shall seek to set the project in the political context of the region. History is for good or ill a real and living thing in Central Europe. Present events that seem obscure often can only be understood against the background of historical events in the region. Ancient hatreds and suspicions are often only just below the surface, waiting to re-emerge. The seismic events of 1989 saw the collapse of communism which had been a restraining influence on nationalism in Central Europe.

The Dam is not just a dam. It is a symbol. That is the key to understanding why the issue has aroused such strong feelings on both sides and why it could easily become a source of regional conflict and instability.

This book is about the politics of the dam. It is not an ecological or economic analysis of the pros and cons of this controversial project. But, we shall need to present the complex economic and environmental arguments deployed by both sides in their unrelenting battle for public opinion at home and even more abroad. The author feels like a Hungarian politician, who recently expressed his exasperation with experts on the dam. He said that he believed them all at one time or another. The author has tried to present these arguments in as balanced and objective fashion as possible and always seeking to provide counter-arguments to any arguments.

The dam, the conflict that it has engendered and its wide political, legal, environmental and economic ramifications are important as a paradigm of modern Central Europe.

J.F.

A Short Chronology of the Dam

1880	First proposals for a hydroelectric dam on the Danube
1920	Trianon Treaty fixes the Danube as the border between Hungary and Slovakia
1952	First talks between Hungary and Czechoslovakia on a dam project
1954	Serious floods in Hungary
1954	Hungarian Water Management Plan recommends a jointly-constructed power dam
1958	Joint Protocol mandates studies
1962 -1977	Planning and studies
1963	COMECON approves the principle of a dam
1977	Treaty signed (September 16)
1978	Construction begins (completion due in 1989)
1980 - 1981	Protests against the dam begin in Hungary
1982	Hungary demands extension of the completion period
1983	Protocol extends completion to 1994
1985	Austrian financing agreed for the Hungarian part
1986	Serious anti-dam protests and marches in Budapest
1988	Hungary demands an acceleration of the project
1989	Protocol sets completion for 1992
1989	Hardi Committee established in Hungary
1989	Hungarian Parliament takes note of the Hardi report and calls for reassessment of the project (October)
1990	Free elections in Hungary and Czechoslovakia
1991	Slovakia invokes Variant C
1991	Fruitless talks and Joint Commission meetings
1992	Hungary unilaterally denounces the Treaty (May)
1992	Elections in Czechoslovakia (June. Break-up of the country becomes inevitable)
1992	Variant C introduced

1992	EC brokers a standstill tripartite agreement
1993	Slovakia and and Czech Republic separate
1993	Case referred to the ICJ in the Hague
1994	Memorials exchanged at the ICJ
1994	Horn Socialist-Liberal coalition in Hungary and the Moravcik government in Slovakia
1995	Basic Agreement signed in Paris (March 1995)

The Dam—Variant C in operation. Photo by John Fitzmaurice.

The Gabčikovo lock. Photo by John Fitzmaurice.

Damming the Danube

1

The Danube: Setting the Scene

The Gabčikovo-Nagymaros dam issue is a complex question involving much more than a massive hydro-electric dam project. It is intimately linked with the River Danube, on which it is located, and with the history and mutual relations of the various peoples in its immediate vicinity. It raises different visions of the river, its future and man's relationship with the river. It involves sensitive issues of ethnic relations in this frontier region and delicate and highly controversial balances between economic and environmental claims.

The Danube flows 2,888 km from its source at Donaueschingen in the German Black Forest to its delta in the Ukranian Black Sea. It is Europe's next largest river, second only to the Volga. Unusually, it effectively flows west to east, not north to south, although in its course, it makes at least two 90° turns. The Danube is certainly Europe's most romantic and mystical river.[1] It is a truly European river, yet also an international river, not just in the legal sense that it is under the surveillance of the International Danube Commission but because it actually flows through no less than ten states. At several different points along its length, it forms an international border. Before 1918, it linked to the great international empires of Central Europe and more recently, flowed between east and west. It passes through areas of Germanic, Slavic and Magyar culture and through settlements of the main European religious faiths: Catholic, Protestant, Orthodox. Despite navigational problems in several reaches, it remains a major trade and transport artery. There is already considerable traffic on the Danube, with a potential for growth into the next century. Some 6 million passengers are carried each year.[2] Its basin is home to 76 million people and it flows through ten cities with more than 100,000 inhabitants, including three capitals (Vienna, Budapest and Belgrade). Even without the Gabčikovo-Nagymaros project, the Danube is already an important energy producer, as the Germans and

Austrians have fully exploited their faster flow sections, with seven power stations. There are also two major dams at the Iron Gates.[3]

As it leaves Austria at Bratislava, the capital of Slovakia ("Pozony" in Hungarian, "Pressburg" in German), the Danube soon becomes part of a complex river system. A right-hand bend (the Moson Danube) leaves the main Danube, runs almost parallel to the Danube, meets the Raab at Györ and runs back into the main river 20 km north of Györ. To the north, the little Danube ("Maly Dunaj" in Slovak) traces a curve of about 100 km and the Váh at Kolarvo and then feeds into the main branch at Komarom. For 140 km, from just beyond Bratislava to just beyond Estergom, the Danube forms the border between Slovakia and Hungary, originally set in the Trianon Treaty of 1920. By its erratic course in this sector, with its many branches and an extensive gravel flood plain, the Danube has created both serious navigation problems in this section between Bratislava and Budapest and a unique natural landscape that would be threatened by works. It is also subject to serious floods, as indeed happened in 1954 and 1965. This section of the Danube, in which the dams are located, has always been problematic. It is a transitional sector in which the river slows down, slackening its gradient and losing its alpine character as it enters its middle section. This has aggravated problems for navigation which have been second only to those in the Iron Gates area. These problems have made intervention tempting though difficult.

A hotly debated issue in relation to the dam project has been the amount of permissible human intervention on the river. Yet, as the above cursory survey of the Danube's significance to the peoples who live along it shows, these have always been competing claims on its resources. This is not a new issue, but the sheer size of the dam project brought these conflicts sharply to the forefront.[4]

The Danube is an internationalised river and has been so since the first Danube Convention in 1856, adopted following the defeat of Russia in the Crimean War. At that time, a European Danube Commission, including non-riparian Great Powers, was established both as a symbol of the river's international status and to ensure free navigation. Following the First World War, the Versailles peace settlement established a new Danube Convention in 1921. An eleven-member international Danube Commission, responsible for navigation from Ulm to Braila (Romania), was set up. It comprised Germany (2 members), Austria, Czechoslovakia, Hungary, Yugoslavia, Bulgaria and Romania for the riparian states, and Britain, France and Italy as representatives of the earlier non-riparian European Danube Commission, deriving from the 1856 Convention. The USSR was excluded.

In the 1930s, as the influence of Fascist Italy and Nazi Germany grew in the region, the international regime was gradually replaced and its organs lost their significance. The powers of the international bodies were re-nationalised. Romania acquired the rights of the commission under the Treaty of Sinaia (1938), to which Germany and Italy acceded. After World War Two, a new Danube regime was needed and a convention was concluded at Belgrade in 1948, to which the by-now communist states alone acceded. The western powers--the United States and the old 1921 signatories--either voted against the convention, abstained or, as in the case of Belgium, Italy and Greece, were not represented. Austria joined the new Danube Commission in 1960. It now has seven members, though clearly the membership will evolve as the situation in relation to the successor states of Czechoslovakia, Yugoslavia and the USSR settles down.[5]

The Gabčikovo-Nagymaros project[6] has generated widespread attention and controversy because of its vast size and because of its implications for the Danube-- one of Europe's most majestic and mythic rivers and a deep and significant part of the European consciousness. It is important to underline the sheer scale of the original project, because human intervention to tame and alter the Danube is by no means new and has certainly not been universally negative. This project is, though, an altogether larger scale. Measures to improve navigability, prevent flooding and harness the river's energy have been undertaken both above and below the sections of the river in which the Gabčikovo-Nagymaros works are situated. Some would argue that there is no longer today any "natural Danube" and so regard the Gabčikovo-Nagymaros plan as a normal and logical continuation of these previous developments.[7] Critics see the Gabčikovo-Nagymaros project as a gigantic and unnecessary intervention. All would agree on the massive scale of the project.

Long discussed in both Czechoslovakia and Hungary, the project[8] was finally agreed upon in a treaty of 1977. With the joint and ancillary national works, it was to represent a massive building programme, extending some 200 km from just below Bratislava to Nagymaros, below the Danube bend and above the Cspel Island, which stretches almost to Budapest. The original project comprised a series of levées on both banks below Bratislava; a large reservoir, 16 km in length, between Hrůsov-Dunakiliti; the Dunakiliti weir itself; the diversion/power canal; the hydro-electric station at Gabičkovo with 8 x 90 mW vertical kaplan turbines and two 34 x 275m navigation locks; the outlet canal meeting the Danube at Palkovičovo; and the Nagymaros power plant, navigation locks and weir. Following the collapse of the communist regime in Hungary, the new government sought to reach a negotiated cancellation of the project with the new democratic authorities in Czechoslovakia. When these negotiations failed, Hungary escalated the dispute by unilaterally terminating the Treaty. Nearly independent Slovakia riposted with Variant C. This temporary solution was put into operation in October 1992. Entirely in Slovak territory, it involves a weir at Cunovo that diverts the water into a now-extended navigation channel down to Gabčikovo and lets a small flow of water into the old river-bed that constitutes the frontier. The Dunakiliti weir (in Hungarian territory) and the Nagymaros works have been discontinued.

Notes

1. For a literary view of the romance and mystery of this great river, see C. Magris *The Danube: Biography of a River*.
2. Pierre Bernard, *Le Roman du Danube*, Paris: Plon, 1991 describes the river from source to mouth. Pp. 115-180 cover the section from Bratislava to Budapest.
3. See the Equipe Cousteau study for the EBRD, entitled *The Danube: For Whom and For What?*, Final Report, March 1993, pp. 69-100.
4. Ibid. p. 104 and pp. 171-172.
5. See S. Gorove, *The Law and Politics of the Danube*, The Hague: 1964, on the international regime of the Danube and its evolution over time.
6. See Equipe Cousteau, *The Danube*, pp. 172-177, for a description of its environmental implications.
7. See J. Liptak, ed., *The Danube: Its Problems and Prospects*, Bratislava: NVK International, 1993, especially pp. 77-96 for a Slovak view.
8. Ministry of Transport, Communications and Public Works of the Slovak Republic, *Commissioning of the Temporary Solution of the Gabčikovo Waterworks*, Bratislava, October 1992, contains a detailed history and specifications of the project.

2

Shaping the Region: 1848-1945

The key to the dam question lies in the difficult relationship between Slovak nationalism and the Czechs and Hungarians. Gabčikovo has become a symbol of Slovak national independence and pride, to be defended equally against Prague and Budapest. One might argue that if the relationships between Bratislava and Budapest and between Bratislava and Prague had been better, then the dam project could have been cancelled in 1990 as both Prague and Budapest actually wanted. In that context, Gabčikovo became an almost unique Slovak victory over both the Czechs and Hungarians.

The Danube region has a complex and conflictual history, and it is only against this background that the present suspicions and conflicts can be understood. The Czechs and Slovaks had separate histories until 1918 when they came together in a common state. They did not know each other, but they needed each other for essentially negative reasons. The Czechs needed the Slovaks as additional Slav "ballast" to balance the German minority. The Slovaks needed a partner to enable them to escape from the domination of Hungary. It proved an unequal and difficult relationship that eventually, after several restarts, led to the (final?) divorce of 1993. The Slovaks therefore always saw two enemies: the Hungarians and the Czechs, neither of whom had accorded them an equal status during their periods of control over Slovakia. Both Czechs and Hungarians were, after 1989, opposed to the Gabčikovo-Nagymaros project, regarding it as a white elephant, a relic of Stalinism. Both would, if it had been left to them, have abandoned the project. For both, the attitude of the Slovaks was the stumbling block. Not surprisingly, the dam issue became part of more generalised mutual misunderstandings, resentments and recriminations. Let us look at this fraught history.

Slovaks were part of Hungary since the early Middle Ages, but the Czech lands, Slovakia and Hungary never were under a single political authority until

1526. Even then, apart from a short period in the mid-nineteenth century, the
Habsburg Empire was never centralised. Indeed, after the Ausgleich in 1867,
the Czechs and Slovaks were in different "halves" of the dual monarchy
established by that Ausgleich.

The Slovaks first appeared in the present area of Slovakia and eastern
Moravia in about 500 AD. The first Slovak state identified as such by many
Slovak nationalist historians was the Greater Moravian Kingdom that came
into being in 840 through the union of the principalities of Nitra and Moravia
under Prince Pribina. It lasted until 907, when it succumbed to Hungarian
attacks that had been intermittently pressed since 895.[1] This kingdom was
important as a national reference point, confirming the Christianisation of the
Slovaks and their western orientation towards Rome rather than Byzantium.
In due course, the Slovaks were incorporated into the Kingdom of St.
Stephan--which was to last until 1918--though as part of the Habsburg
possessions after 1526, following the defeat of the Hungarians by the Turks
at the Battle of Mohács. Most of Hungary, but only the eastern part of
Slovakia, was occupied by the Turks until the Treaty of Karlowitz in 1699.[2]

For much of the eighteenth century, Upper Hungary, as Slovakia was
called, became the centre of political life in Hungary with the capital in
Bratislava and the seat of the Hungarian primate in Estergom. Earlier, in
1635, a Jesuit university had been founded at Trnava, becoming the centre of
the early Slovak national renaissance. Following the first real codification of
the Slovak language by Daniel Krman (1740) and Pavol Dolezal (1746), the
university sponsored a translation of the Bible in 1756-59 and the work of
Anton Bernolák (1762-1813), with his Disertatio philologico-critica de litteris
slovarum (1887) and dictionary published in 1825-27 after his death. His
work was continued by the historian-politician and writer Ludovit Stur, who
developed the Slovak literary language based on the central Slovak dialect.
Other Protestant nationalists such as Jan Kollar were pan-Slavs and continued
to use and propagate the Czech language.[3]

The upsurge of nationalism (Magyar, German and Slav) and with it the
1848 revolutions in Germany, Austria and Hungary posed a dilemma and
some difficult choices for the Slovak national movement. Should it join the
pan-Slav movement? Should it assert its distinctiveness? How should it react
to the revolution in Hungary? The leaders of the Slovak movement did attend
the first Pan-Slav Congress in Prague in 1848, called as riposte to the
Frankfurt German Parliament, then the rallying point of the pan-Germanist
movement.[4] The congress was divided and was soon dispersed by Imperial
troops.[5] In parallel, the Slovak nationalists prepared their demands for

autonomy within Hungary and above all, a reversal of the language laws adopted in 1830 and 1847 that made the Hungarian language the only official language of the Kingdom. The Manifesto adopted at Liptovskysvaty Mikulas on May 10, 1848, and addressed to the Emperor and the Hungarian parliament, asked for the creation of distinct Slovak administrative districts, the right to use the Slovak language, Slovak representation in parliament and basic civil rights, such as the freedom of the press.[6] As the Hungarian revolution intensified under Lajos Kossuth, a radical nationalist, it became less and less likely that there would be any Hungarian willingness to compromise on the concept of autonomy, let alone federalism, as proposed by the Pan-Slav Congress.[7] Indeed, Kossuth himself was the author of the 1847 language laws. As so often in the region, two nationalisms were in direct conflict.

Slovakia now faced the radicalisation of Hungarian nationalism that led to the Declaration of Independence by the government in Debrecen. At this point, the Slovak leaders chose, like the Croatians under Jelačic, to throw in their lot with the Austrians, in the ultimately vain hope that they could extract concessions, once the Hungarian revolution had been crushed.

Initially, there was some willingness on the part of Austrian leaders to seek a compromise with the nationalists. In March 1849, the Emperor received a 28-member delegation at Olomouc and seriously considered its representations, at least on limited autonomy.[8] Following the proclamation of Hungarian Independence on April 14, 1849, the Emperor accepted the Russian Tsar's offer of assistance, and the revolt was crushed by Russian forces at Vilagos in August 1849. This was also the end of attempts to reach a compromise with the Slovaks.

In the next fifteen years, there was a complex and tortuous series of attempts to find a new constitutional structure for the Empire. The liberalism and moderate constitutionalism of the 1849 constitution were abandoned in favour of a neo-absolutist centralism.[9] The Crown lands of St. Stephan ceased to be a distinct political entity within the Empire. Hungarian tariffs and tax systems were abolished and the old Comitats were replaced by new "rationalised" administrative districts.[10] After the Austrian defeat in Italy in 1859, the regime was weakened and Hungarian nationalists began to reemerge, forcing re-establishment of the pre-1848 Hungarian constitution.[11]

The 1859 and 1861 constitutional laws were the basis for the 1867 Ausgleich. For the first time, the outlines of a dualist scheme were perceptible. The "narrow" Reichsrat (without Hungarian representatives) was to deal with matters of concern to the non-Hungarian part of the Empire. Local Diets were to deal with local matters and the full Reichsrat would deal with matters of common concern to the whole Empire. This was a solution of dualism and centralism: dualism between the Austrian and Hungarian parts of the Empire and centralism within the non-Hungarian Crown lands.[12]

However, the system was not yet fully dualist, nor was this the intention of Vienna. As a result, it was not acceptable to any but those of the most conservative opinion in Hungary and was rejected by the Diet in Budapest in April 1861.[13] Nor was the centralist cast of the system acceptable to Czechs.[14] The address by the Hungarian Diet rejected the system, but did not burn all the bridges. As it was, both the full and narrow Reichsrat was boycotted by the Czechs, Croatians, Poles and even the Tyrolians. This was the position when the war broke out between Austria and Prussia in 1866. The Empire faced strains and the need to come to terms with Hungary on a new basis, recognising the Hungarians and the Germans as its two pillars or "Staatsvölker."

The national revolution in Hungary had only been defeated with extreme difficulty, even with Russian military assistance at Vilagos. There was a real but unfounded fear that the Hungarian moderates might be outflanked. There was also concern that the revolutionary republicans might recover their position in an objective alliance with Prussia during the prolonged battle for supremacy in Germany, which culminated in Austria's defeat in the short war with Prussia in 1866. Indeed, Prussia did form Hungarian nationalist military units. They played only a very modest part in actual hostilities, but were highly symbolic.[15]

Out of these concerns came the Ausgleich, agreed between the new Premier, Count Beul, and the moderate Hungarian nationalist leaders, Count Andrassy and Istvan Deak. The Ausgleich established the dual monarchy, which was declared to be a real union, going beyond a mere personal union of two kingdoms. Each half had its own government and institutions, and domestic affairs--including matters of policy relating to minorities--were dealt with by each half of the monarchy. There were also joint institutions to manage common affairs. There were common Ministers of Foreign Affairs, War and Finance. There was a common Cabinet Council of the three joint Ministers and the two Prime Ministers, chaired by the Joint Foreign Minister. The Hungarian contribution to joint expenditure was set at a very favourable 30 percent, to be renegotiated every ten years on renewal of the Ausgleich. It never rose above 36.4 percent. In addition, some economic matters such as tariffs and communications, though administered separately, were subject to joint rules agreed to for a period of ten years at each renewal. Each side incorporated those provisions into its own constitutional legislation. There was no common parliament, but delegations made up of representatives of each parliament met annually, alternately in Vienna and Budapest to deal with common matters.[16]

The Hungarians adopted a one-sided interpretation of the Ausgleich that was never challenged or at least never overridden by the Austrian side. The Hungarians claimed that the Ausgleich was conditional on the maintenance of constitutional government in Austria. That might in itself have been reasonable, but their interpretation of this concept was that the structure of the Austrian half of the dual monarchy must remain as it had been in 1867. Indeed, this view was pressed successfully against a Czech-Austrian Ausgleich in 1871 and was the formal pretext for dissolution of the dual monarchy in 1918 following Emperor Karl's federalist manifesto.[17]

The Habsburg Empire was perhaps temporarily shored up by the Ausgleich by basing it on the dualist hegemony of its German and Hungarian peoples, but the ultimate fate of the Empire was sealed. Reform was impossible. The Emperor could not intervene to respond to the pressure of Slav nationalities such as the Slovaks, Croatians and Slovenians in Hungary. Nor could a solution be found to the problem of nationalities that lived in both halves. Despite the apparent mutual non-interference in internal affairs, this had become a one-way street. The Hungarians were accorded an effective veto over reforms in the Austrian half, preventing the conclusion of the Ausgleich with the Czechs.

Inevitably, Czech political opinion evolved and became more radicalised. In the 1840s, the great Czech historian Palacky said that if the Habsburg Empire did not exist, it would be necessary to invent it. In 1867, he himself went to the Second Pan-Slav Congress. In the 1860s, the Old Czech party under its conservative leadership, including Francis Rieger, argued for the traditional Staatsrecht of the old Bohemian Crown (Bohemia, Moravia, Silesia), which could have been enshrined in a second Czech-Austrian Ausgleich after 1867.[18]

This would have been included in a package of measures. It had two pillars: the language legislation based on a liberal application of Article 19 of the 1867 organic law on the constitutional rights of citizens and, secondly, the so-called fundamental articles for political reform. Under the proposals put forward by Prime Minister Von Hohenwart, Bohemia would have achieved far-reaching autonomy in economic and cultural matters by being placed under the Bohemian Chancellery and a Bohemian Diet with two curias (one Czech and one German). Bohemian deputies would sit not in the Austrian Cisleithian

Reichsrat but in a congress of delegates from both bodies to deal with remaining joint matters.

Article 19 of the Constitutional law had already laid down the principle that each ethnic group had equal rights and "the right to preserve and cultivate its nationality and language."[19] The equality of customary languages in education, administration and political life in each of the Crown lands (in Cisleithan Austria) was recognised as was the right to establish ethnic schools supported by public funds. The Reichsgericht was established to hear appeals arising from the application of these principles. The Czech Ausgleich package then proposed the creation of nationally homogenous administrative districts, equality of the Czech language everywhere, with the requirement that officials should have command of both languages and separate cultural budgets. This was a reasonable compromise and as such was attacked from both the German and Czech nationalist standpoint.

However, it was not this internal opposition that sank the package. It floundered on the opposition of the Hungarians. Prime Minister Andrassy argued that it was contrary to the Hungarian Ausgleich. At the same time, the German Emperor intervened to object on the grounds that it was contrary to the interests of the German nationalists. These combined pressures led the Emperor and his Cabinet to back down.[20] The moderation of the old Czech leaders was ill-repaid as the Czechs were sacrificed at the altar of reconciliation with Hungary and Germany, a short-sighted attitude that blighted all hope of an overall resolution of the nationalities problems. All could now see that the empire could not deliver. Radicalisation of Czech opinion inevitably followed, and the implications were not lost on other nationalities, such as the South Slavs, Ruthenians, Italians and Romanians, whose fate depended on the same or similar balancing of considerations.

The Old Czech Party found itself increasingly bypassed by the Young Czechs under the brilliant leadership of Karel Kramar. By the 1880s, the Young Czechs dominated politics in the Czech lands. They were moderately pan-Slav and nationalist, finding their support among urban voters. By 1897, they too declined, as new parties emerged (Masaryk's Realist Party and the later National Socialist Party) that had a better grasp of social as well as national issues. In fact, national, social and religious questions were closely intertwined in Bohemia.[21]

A second, less ambitious attempt to achieve some pacification in the Czech lands also failed. Bypassing the Reichsrat, the Badenyi government used the emergency procedure to adopt two language degrees for Moravia in 1897. These provided that throughout the Bohemian Crown lands, both Czech and

German could be used before the courts and in the administration. Within three years, officials would have to master both languages. In reality, this only posed a problem for German-speaking officials, as the Czechs already spoke German adequately. The German deputies in the Reichsrat hindered and eventually killed these not unreasonable measures by filibuster, disorder and parliamentary obstruction on other matters.[22]

At the turn of the century, Socialist leader Karl Renner (later Chancellor and President of the Second Austrian Republic) proposed an ingenious solution based on the concept of personal autonomy. Under his proposals, a person's ethnic status would become an individual matter, rather than a geographical one. National status would have been accorded to individuals who would make up cultural communities that would be accorded rights by the state, irrespective of where their members actually geographically resided. The authority of such bodies would be non-territorial. This non-geographical federalism could deal with the problems of mixed and dispersed nationalities within the overall framework of the Empire. This is the essence of the modern Belgian approach. Indeed, this method was applied in Moravia in 1905; in Bukovina between Ruthenians, Jews, Romanians and Germans (1910); and between Poles and Ruthenians in Galocia in 1913. Interesting and relatively successful through these schemes were, they were too limited, too little and too late. In any case, they were all implemented only in the Cisleithian half of the monarchy and so could not resolve the problems raised by the South Slavs, Italians, the Slovaks or the bulk of the Romanians.[23]

In Hungary, the situation of the Slovaks was even more difficult than that of the Czechs. Like all the nationalities within the Hungarian part of the Empire (except the Croatians, who achieved their own partial Ausgleich in 1868), the Slovaks were abandoned to their fate and could no longer appeal outside the Hungarian state to Vienna for redress. Such a possibility was now no longer even theoretically available to them.

The Slovaks faced a repressive Magyarisation policy that saw their schools and cultural organisations suppressed and their political representation denied. The Hungarian language was imposed as the only official language. This repression intensified in the 1870s. The Slovak Cultural Institute (Matica Slovenska) was closed in 1875. The number of Slovak primary schools fell from 1,921 in 1869 to 440 in 1911. The number of hours of Hungarian-language instruction in these schools was raised to twenty. There were never more than seven Slovaks elected to the Hungarian Parliament at one time, and in 1869, 1875, 1878 and 1881, none was elected. There were several small riots in Slovakia and several hundred Slovaks were, as a result, imprisoned for political activities.[24]

Slovak leaders did what they could to maintain their culture and their language, as well as whatever political or quasi-political organisation was possible within the constraints of the system. Numerous cultural and literary associations were established, such as the University of Bratislava (Academia Istropolitana), whose origins dated back to the reign of Mathias Corvinus (1458-90); the Jesuit University of Trnava (1635); the Slovak Academy in Trnava (1792); the Protestant Literary Society in Bratislava (1803); the Literary Association of the Banska Slavnica Region (1812); the Bratislava University Students' Association (1827); and the Tatrin Cultural and Youth Education Society in 1844. Two Protestant and one Catholic grammar schools were founded in the 1860s, only to close a decade later. The most important association was the Matica Slovenska (1863) with the Catholic Bishop Moyses as Chairman and the Protestant Pastor Kuzmány as Vice-Chairman. It even received a subsidy from the Emperor. It was established in Turčiansky St. Martin, the cultural and political centre of Slovak nationalism.[25]

On the political level, cultural leaders such as Ludovit Stur, Milan Hodža and Jozef Hurban were at various times also elected as deputies. A Slovak national assembly was held in Turčiansky St. Martin on June 6-7, 1861, which adopted the Memorandum of the Slovak Nation,[26] an autonomist political platform. After the Ausgleich, there was less and less space for open and legal Slovak nationalist political activity, thought the Slovak National Party was founded in 1868 and the Slovak People's Party in 1905.[27] A different, mainly Protestant, "Czechslovakist" tendency called Hlassite after the journal of that movement, Hlass ("Voice"), developed. This group was in close contact with T.G. Masaryk, the Czech leader, and worked within the Czechoslovenska Jednota (Czechoslovak Union), founded in 1898 for a Union of Czechs, Moravians and Slovaks in the struggle against Magyarisation and Germanisation.[28]

The First World War radically altered the situation in the region. Initially, neither the Allies[29] nor the Slav minorities sought the dismemberment of the dual monarchy and the creation of national states, but as the war continued, positions radicalised.[30] Indeed, serious divergences between the emigré Czech leadership and the Czech parliamentarians within the Empire continued until almost the end of the War. As late as 1917, when the Reichsrat was reopened, the Czech deputies' statement called for no more than a multinational federation. It was only the collapse of the secret talks aimed at a separate peace between Vienna and the Allies and the disappearance of the autocratic Tsarist ally after the Bolshevik revolution that opinion both among the emigrés, the Allies and nationalist leaders within shifted towards the national state solution, on the basis of Wilsonian self-determination.[31] In June 1918, the French government, followed by the other Allies, recognized the Czech National Council, and President Wilson reinterpreted point ten of his fourteen points as meaning independent statehood for the minorities in the Empire. France became a champion of strong Czech, Polish and South Slav states as part of a system of alliances, supporting the post-war status quo and a cordon sanitaire against both Germany and the Soviet Union, the most dangerous potential revisionists.[32]

Where did Slovakia come in? For the French and the Czechs, a Czech state was too small and weak and would contain too large a German minority compared with the Czech population. One solution was a Czechoslovak Union.[33] For the Slovaks themselves, there were three options: an intra-Hungarian solution, a Slovak state or a Czecho-Slovak federal union. Slovak politics in the United States became the nerve centre of the national movements in the early years of the century.[34] The Jednota (Union), led by Father Furdek and the Slovak National Society under Peter Rovnianek, came together in 1909 to form the American Slovak League. Gradually, its views evolved towards cooperation with the Czech National Council. This cooperation led to signature of the Cleveland Agreement in October 1915, which called for a "union of the Czech and Slovak nations in a Federation of States, with full autonomy for Slovakia."[35] A second agreement, the Pittsburgh Convention of May 30, 1918, affirmed the same principles, but more vaguely: "We approve the political program for a Union of the Czechs and Slovaks in an independent state. Slovakia will have its own Administration, Parliament and Judiciary."[36]

In October 1918, the government in exile and the Czech National Council in Prague declared the Independence of Czechoslovakia. The Slovak General Stefanik was a member of the provisional government in France. The Slovaks in Hungary held a secret session of the National Council, representing all Slovak parties and on October 30, 1918, adopted the Declaration of Turčiansky St. Martin. The provisional Hungarian government offered them no viable intra-Hungarian solution, even if the Allies would have accepted such an approach. In any case, an independent Slovakia on its own would not easily survive revisionist Hungarian pressures. The Declaration therefore opted for the solution of a Czechoslovak Union. The text is imprecise as to the form of the state and fails to use the terms federation or autonomy, unlike the Cleveland agreement. This was a fatal error.[37]

In the last months of the War, there was a rapid acceleration of diplomatic developments and chaos on the ground in Central Europe, as at long last the Empire came apart at the seams. What actually happened depended on a mixture of policy design and the situation as it evolved. As it was, the Allies, France in the van, came to favour the dissolution of the Empire and its transformation into national states that would replace Russia as France's eastern ally and form a bulwark both against Germany and Bolshevik Russia. This, of course, had not been the original Allied intention. In any case, as we shall see, events on the ground went far towards making preservation of the Empire impossible in any form.

By the time the War ended, the Czechoslovak state had already been proclaimed, on October 28, and it was fighting to establish its territory. The new state was surrounded by enemies. Austria sought to retain the German-populated Sudetenland. Hungary sought to retain part of Slovakia. The communist threat from Russia and later from the Hungarian-Socialist Republic was omnipresent. Even Poland, a fellow successor state, had claims on the ore-rich Teschen area. It should be remembered that the Allied great powers had no large bodies of troops in Central Europe.

Internally, there were centralists, descendants of the Hlassites and Slovak autonomists. The communists were soon to emerge as a force opposed to the Czechoslovak state until 1938. There were two broad tendencies within the Czech leadership: the internal pan-Slav tendency led by Karel Kramar, Czechoslovakia's first Prime Minister, and the external, western-oriented tendency led by President Masaryk and Foreign Minister Beneš.

Kramar looked east to Russia for support, whereas Masaryk looked to the western democracies. For Kramar, the best solution was a Central European Slavic federation under Russian leadership. Masaryk sought a western-orientated, liberal democratic Republic. Both made contacts in their preferred directions during the early part of the War. Their respective orientations affected the boundaries they proposed for the new state. Kramar proposed an "enlarged" Bohemia of about 15 million, which would take in parts of Saxony and Prussia (Lusatia lost in the Middle Ages) and would extend Slovakia further into Hungary and meet Serbia. Masaryk, on the other hand, wanted above all a viable state with defensible natural borders based both on the historic Czech Crown lands--Bohemia, Moravia, Silesia and, for ethnic reasons, Slovakia. His programme was a pragmatic synthesis of historic and ethnic claims extended to take on board some, but not all of Kramar's claims, together with strategic demands relating to the Teschen coalfields and a corridor through western Hungary to the Slav successor state of Yugoslavia.[38]

But these ideas had to be fought for at Versailles. The peace conference never took a general overview of central Europe's problems and future development.[39] The Wilsonian principles proved an inadequate practical guide, conflicting as they often did both with the interests of other great powers and with the complexity of the situation on the ground. Only France had a clear vision of what it wanted: a barrier of strong successor states from the Baltic to the Adriatic, in alliance with France, as upholders of the peace settlement and bulwarks against a resurgent Germany, Bolshevik Russia and revisionist Hungary and Austria. Apart from a brief flirtation with Hungary, France stuck to this line throughout the peace conference. It was also the line of Masaryk, so Czechoslovakia normally received preferential French support. In the Teschen dispute, matters were less clear as Poland was also a key factor in the French chain of successor states. France therefore in large measure imposed its view, both in the Czechoslovak Commission and in the full conference. Thus, both the Versailles Treaty, the St. Germain Treaty (Austria) and the Trianon Treaty (Hungary), plus the subsequent Teschen settlement were favourable to Czechoslovakia.[40]

The deferred price--paid in 1938--was a combination of internal instability and external isolation that eventually destroyed Czechoslovakia, the nearest thing to a liberal democracy in eastern Europe, in the inter-war period. As one observer aptly summarised the situation: "Czechoslovakia, instead of being a part of a large pro-western, anti-German chain of states, became an island in a sea of hostile forces, unable to rely on any of its neighbours for help. This encirclement, first apparent in late 1919 and in 1920, was never successfully broken by Czech foreign policy."[41]

Closely interrelated, internal problems were no less difficult. Initially, the Allies used the term "Union" in early drafts of the Treaties of St. Germain and Trianon and even in the final text called the new state Czecho-Slovakia (with a hyphen). Despite the apparent acceptance of a federalist or unionist form for the new state, the dominant Czech leadership failed to deliver on its commitments.[42] Of course, in the face of large, non-Czechoslovak minorities --German, Hungarian, Ruthenian--a strong centralised state seemed necessary. A federation also would have been a precedent for these other minorities.

The Czech First Republic (1918-1939) made mistakes in dealing with the minority issue, but it was the nearest there was to a democratic state in Central Europe. Indeed, in the stable middle period of the life of the First Republic, there was relatively good cooperation between political parties and nationalities, which made the state governable in a way that it ceased to be by the late 1930s. It was the external pressures from Nazi Germany that destabilised the Czechoslovak state by offering new and tempting opportunities to its dissatisfied minorities, essentially the Germans, Slovaks and Hungarians. It might have been a more sensible policy to have sought an earlier and broader accommodation with them, in which case these opportunities might have seemed less attractive.

The Czech leadership did make efforts to reach a compromise with the German parties in the early years of the Republic over the constitution and over minority issues, but it failed. Only when it became clear that the Czechoslovak state was there to stay did the Germans change their stance. After 1926, representatives of the German Agrarians and Socialists entered the Cabinet. It was not until 1935, after Hitler came to power, that extreme nationalists--Henlein's Sudeten-partei--won a majority among Germans. Earlier, the Nazis and nationalists had been a small minority (under 20 percent) of the German vote. Clearly, after 1935, the pro-Czechoslovak parties among the German community lost all legitimacy.[43]

There were some parallels in Slovakia. Some Slovaks, particularly Protestants, were centralists and "Czechoslovakists." Others sought to defend the long-term Slovak demands for autonomy. Thus, in 1938, 35 of the 58 Slovak deputies signed an autonomist statement. As in the Sudetenland, the process of polarisation was gradual.

At first, Andrej Hlinka, leader of the Slovak Populist Party, supported the Czechoslovak state, but he gradually moved into opposition. In 1925, his party won only 34 percent of the Slovak vote, but this increased to 50 percent by 1935. Eventually, only the Slovak outposts of the national parties served in the central government and supported the Union, and they were increasingly a minority in Slovakia.[44]

With over 20 significant parties and in effect three distinct party systems (Sudeten, national and Slovak) that became increasingly centrifugal and confrontational, it became difficult to construct majorities based on broad consensus and with equal legitimacy in the German, Czech and Slovak communities. The situation in Slovakia was aggravated by the pressures from the Hungarian minority, supported by Hungary. This situation could only be made worse when, as after 1932, an external force exercised pressure on Czechoslovakia through the German minority. As Konrad Henlein, the Sudeten leader put it, 70 million Germans stood behind the 3 million Sudeten Germans. This could only encourage the other revisionists internally and externally.

There are certainly two readings of the collapse of the First Czechoslovakian Republic. The Czech view was that the Slovak nationalists sought a deliberate confrontation with the central authorities after Munich and after the occupation of the rest of the Czech lands (Bohemia and Moravia) in March 1939. This provoked first the suspension of the Slovak government and then the secession of Slovakia with German support and encouragement, creating an authoritarian collaborationist state that lasted until 1945.

The other view, widely held in Slovakia, and not completely rejected even by Slovak communists, was that the persistent failure of the dominant Czech political class of the First Republic to honour the founding compact of the new Czechoslovak nation, namely that the Slovaks should enjoy equality and significant autonomy, if not federalism, had led to a situation that rendered the conduct of the Slovak nationalists justified and not treasonable. In this view, the collapse of the Czechoslovak state was a legitimate opportunity to create a Slovak state, even if it did come into existence with the support of Nazi Germany.

Reality is more complex and balanced, offering some support to both views. Certainly, as we have seen, the position of Slovakia within the First Czechoslovakian Republic was not satisfactory. As in other multi-ethnic states threatened by Germany during the Second World War, such as Yugoslavia or Belgium, there was an obvious temptation for the Slovaks to use the external threat to break the stranglehold of the dominant Czech nationality, even if this meant a degree of collaboration with the German enemy of Czechoslovakia. For the dominant group that controlled the old state, such behaviour was treason, but treason towards a state that Slovaks, or Flemish or Croats, rejected.

There were parallel internal developments. Even before the Munich agreement, the various non-Czech nationalities had begun to cooperate to achieve a decentralisation or federalisation of the Czechoslovakian state. Thus, on September 8, 1938, the political committee of the Sudetendeutsche Partei (the dominant Sudeten German party), the Hungarian and Polish parties and the Slovaks established a coordination agreement aimed at restructuring the state.[45]

As we have seen, earlier attempts at constitutional reform--in 1925 and 1930--had failed.[46] Without being consulted, Slovakia was obliged, under the first Vienna Award that followed the Munich agreement, to cede the southern Danubian strip of territory to Hungary. In reaction, all Slovak political parties, except the communists, now came together to support the position of the Slovak People's Party (the largest) in favour of a federation. Thus, 35 out of 50 Slovak deputies adhered to the Declaration of Zilna on October 6, 1938, forming a common front under the national union label and calling for immediate autonomy.[47]

On November 19, 1938, the Parliament in Prague finally endorsed a reform of the constitution, establishing a federal state of Bohemia-Moravia, Slovakia and sub-Carpathian Ruthenia. Serious disputes however remained over the replacement of some 9,000 Czech officials in Slovakia and over Slovakia's contribution to common services. The new federal state, bereft of both Sudetenland and the Danube valley, was weak and vulnerable to outside revisionist predators such as the Third Reich and Hungary.

Naturally, the Munich crisis and then the occupation of rump Bohemia in March 1939 created a new political situation. Slovakia faced difficult choices: occupation by Germany or annexation by Hungary, a revisionist ally of Germany and Italy seeking to reverse the territorial losses of the Trianon Treaty. It should not be forgotten that before 1918, Slovakia had been part of the Hungarian Kingdom in the dual monarchy. The Czechoslovak government went back on the agreement to decentralise the state and on March 10, 1939, removed the Slovak government that had been set up under that agreement.

Prime Minister Tiso was invited to Berlin to meet with Adolf Hitler, for whom this internal crisis was a welcome prelude to his own intervention to take over Bohemia and Moravia. Monsignor Tiso was faced with a "coup de théâtre": evidence that in parallel Hungary intended to occupy the rest of Slovakia. Hitler demanded that Slovakia declare independence under German protection or else be left to its fate.

The least worst solution was to declare Slovakia independent, which the Slovak Diet did on March 14, 1939. Hungary was then awarded sub-Carpathian Ruthenia. Czechoslovakia had ceased to exist.[48]

Who was at fault? The question remains controversial to this day. Certainly, Czech policy before 1938 had done little to justify Slovak loyalty to the common Czechoslovak state. However, Czechs and Slovaks were in the end victims of Nazi policy. Independence in a client state remained a better solution, whatever the negative characteristics of the Slovak state, than Hungarian or German occupation.

The Slovak state was recognised by a large number of foreign governments: 29 in all. Apart from the Axis states, Slovakia was recognised by Britain on May 4, 1939; Poland on March 15, 1939; France on July 14, 1939; Belgium on September 11, 1939; the Soviet Union on September 16, 1939; Switzerland on April 19, 1939. The only significant country not to recognise the new Slovak state was the United States.[49] Slovakia was obliged to conclude an alliance with Germany on March 23, 1939. Under this treaty, Germany guaranteed Slovak independence, whilst Slovakia aligned itself with the Axis, as its participation in the war against the USSR with two armoured divisions was to clearly demonstrate.[50]

The new Constitution was adopted on July 21, 1939. Under it, the President was elected by Parliament for seven years. An 80-member parliament and a 9-member Cabinet were established. The system was, in theory, a Liberal parliamentary one. In reality, the political system rapidly became authoritarian. The Executive became dominant at the expense of Parliament. The communist and socialist parties were suppressed and the other Slovak parties were formed into a united front.[51] Only the small German and Hungarian minority parties remained. Gradually, all real power was concentrated in the hands of Monsignor Tiso, the strong man of the regime who was elected President.

In the 1930s, the Slovak national movement was not overtly Fascist. It was nationalist, anti-Czech, anti-Hungarian, Conservative and Catholic. Hence, the "Clerical-Fascist" description found in some literature.[52] In the wake of the foundation of the Unified Party, then the secession of Slovakia in 1939--and with it the closer links with Nazi Germany--the more radical rightist and pro-Nazi wing of the movement gained the upper hand, under the umbrella of the leader, Monsignor Tiso. The leaders from the right, such as Premier Tuka, Mach (Interior Minister) and Durčansky (all members of the Hlinka Guard, a fascist militia), were separatist, authoritarian and anti-semitic. Under the umbrella of a common commitment to nationalism, these diverse groups remained in the fold. In the end, the regime could not resist German pressure: 53,000 Slovak Jews were deported.

Inevitably, the Slovak state could not survive the demise of its German patron. Slovakia, like Croatia and the would-be Flemish state, could only expect to survive if Germany won the war. By late 1944, the Red Army was closing in on the borders of Slovakia. Already, Soviet agents and parachutists had linked up with the internal resistance, made up of communists, socialists and liberals. In early September 1944, the Slovak National Rising was launched at Banská Bystrica and a Democratic Slovak Republic was briefly created. It took the Germans two months of bloody repression, in which 30,000 Slovaks were killed, to quell the uprising.[53] Slovakia was then liberated by the Red Army and not by its own efforts--a key political distinction--in April 1945. The national Czechoslovak government under

President Beneš returned to the country and established itself in Košice in eastern Slovakia.

The failure of the uprising and the liberation of Slovakia by the Red Army ensured that there could be no Slovak state, not even a democratic one. Indeed, on the diplomatic front, the Allied leadership, including Stalin, had already given their support to the restoration of the old Czechoslovak state by agreeing to void the Munich agreement and other changes, including the Slovak secession and the Vienna award. The Czechoslovak state was to be re-established within its pre-1938 borders, except for Ruthenia, which was ceded to the USSR.

In addition to securing the support of the western Allies and their agreement to void the Munich agreement, President Beneš adopted a quite different approach to the Soviet Union to that of the Polish exile leaders and indeed was encouraged in that policy by Churchill. This was in line with the desire of the western Allies to secure and cement the Grand Alliance with Stalin against Nazi Germany. President Beneš had concluded that the Soviet Union was going to be the dominant power in the region after the defeat of Germany. The best hope for Czechoslovakia lay in forging close relations with the USSR and doing so while the war was still going on. This was both realistic and actually far less at variance with public sentiment at least in the Czech lands than it would have been in Poland. Czechoslovakia, with its large German and Hungarian minorities, needed the strong protector that it had not had in 1938. Indeed, for many Czechs, the western betrayal at Munich was a sharp lesson, that deterred them from placing too much reliance on the western democracies. The Soviet alliance, and with it an internal compromise with the Communist Party, offered an additional advantage. It would enable the Czechoslovak government both to restore a relatively centralised state and to deal with the German and Hungarian minorities in a severely radical and punitive manner by large-scale expulsions. This required both broad internal consensus and Allied support.[54]

The government in exile in London was recognised by Britain on July 18, 1941, and by the United States on July 31. The exile government concluded its first agreement with the United States as early as July 1941. Under this agreement, the redrawn borders of 1938 and 1939 were declared void. Britain and the United States followed suit in 1942. As the partners of war shifted and the liberation of Czechoslovakia from the east became a real possibility, President Beneš visited Moscow, and on December 12, 1943, signed a Treaty of Friendship with the USSR. The Czechoslovakian government in exile had gained Allied support for its policy of re-establishment of the former Czechoslovak state within the 1938 borders and for the expulsion of at least part of the anti-Czech German and Hungarian minorities. This restoration also could ignore the decentralising concessions made to the Slovaks under pressure in 1939. Indeed, Beneš himself pressed Molotov and Stalin in Moscow in December 1943 to demand measures against the Slovak collaborators after the war. This would be his alibi. Molotov well understood that this meant giving the Czechs carte blanche to restore the status quo ante.[55]

Hungary was the biggest loser after World War One. Under the Treaty of Trianon, it lost two-thirds of its territory and its population fell from 20.8 million in 1910 to 8.5 million after the war. Before the war, it was a multinational kingdom. The dominant Hungarian nationality was only 48.1 percent of the total population. The Slovaks were 9.8 percent. After the war, the new Hungarian state was 90 percent Hungarian, having lost Slovakia, Transylvania, the Banat, Croatia and Slovonia.[56]

Hungary's foreign policy was based on revisionism and anti-Communism. It became the prime revisionist state with Austria and Italy, with whom it sought an alliance against the French-inspired pro-Versailles-settlement Little Entente powers (Yugoslavia, Romania, Czechoslovakia and Poland). In the early 1930s, before the sealing of the Berlin-Rome axis between Mussolini and Hitler, the Italians and Hungarians also opposed the growing German influence in the region. After the Anschluss on March 19, 1938, it became clear that the revisionist powers had no alternative to the German alliance and that indeed by means of that alliance, they might realise at least part of their revisionist goals.[57] Hungary was able, in the two Vienna Awards, to annexe the most Hungarian areas of Slovakia along the Danube and in northern Transylvania, as well as Ruthenia. Later, after the dismemberment of Yugoslavia, it gained the Voivodina. The price of this alliance was increasing economic, political and military subordination to Germany and participation in the Russian campaign from 1941. Despite attempts to remain neutral in the earlier part of the war, Hungary was obliged to commit two full armies to the eastern front and suffered severe losses, for example, in the Battle of Stalingrad. As early as 1942, Hungary sought to disengage from the German alliance and even opened secret talks with the western powers. Its closeness to Germany and its strategic importance meant that its attempts to opt out of the war were doomed (unlike Romania) to failure. German forces entered the country in March 1944 and a pro-German Cabinet was imposed on the Regent. As Soviet forces approached Hungarian territory, Admiral Horthy sought to organise a coup similar to that engineered by the King of Romania.

The Germans acted decisively. Horthy was removed to Germany and a Fascist and strongly anti-semitic government was installed under Ferenc Szalasi, leader of the extremist Arrow Cross Movement.[58] As the Red Army liberated eastern Hungary, a provisional government was established in Debrecen. Budapest was under siege from December 25, 1944, until February 13, 1945. Fighting in Hungary continued until early April 1945.

Hungarian domestic policy during the inter-war period was complex and at times chaotic, swinging from extreme left to far right in a short compass. Hungary was the main loser at the Paris Peace Conference. Among the main Allied powers, only Italy was inclined to support it against its Slav neighbours, Yugoslavia, Czechoslovakia and Romania, all of whom had received promises of Hungarian territory. All were vital parts of the French grand design for a central European barrier against German resurgence and against Bolshevism. Hungary was involved in military conflict with both Czechoslovakia and Romania, as these successor states sought to create a fait accompli. It faced increasing territorial demands, backed by the Allies, and economic collapse and famine.

Without support from the west, the moderate government of Count Karolyi collapsed in March 1919 and was replaced by a communist Soviet government under Bela Kun, which was not recognised by the Allies, but with which they nevertheless sought in vain to reach some accommodation. However, Bela Kun's regime was short-lived. He was overthrown by nationalists operating from the Szeged region. The country was then occupied by French troops under Admiral Horthy and by a Romanian invasion that controlled Budapest. Elections held by the new provisional government of the populist Huszár in January 1920 led to a victory for the centre-right National Christian Party and the Small Landowners' Party in a coalition under the close tutelage of the military. There followed a complex battle over the form of the state, with Hungary becoming a monarchy without a king under Horthy as Regent in March 1920, as the Allies opposed any restoration of the Habsburg Dynasty. Following two tragic-comic restoration attempts by the former Emperor Karl in 1921, the Regency remained until Horthy was removed in the later stages of the Second World War.

Domestically, Hungary became a only limited parliamentary democracy, as the role of the Regent and the army remained considerable and voting was not secret in the countryside until 1939. Socialists were regularly elected to Parliament in the 1920s and 1930s, and it was not until 1944 quite a totalitarian state. Hungary remained inevitably strongly nationalist and revisionist, reaching no rapprochement with its Slav neighbours and indeed taking part in the dismemberment of Czechoslovakia in 1938-39. Internally, it adopted, as in the nineteenth century, a policy of forced assimilation towards the Slav minorities that remained within its Trianon borders.[59]

Not surprisingly, both Czechoslovakia and Hungary were both internally unstable, threatened from outside and manipulated instruments of the Great Powers in the inter-war period. Czechoslovakia failed to become the lynchpin, as France had envisaged, in a Slav bloc allied to France. It remained wedged between hostile states that claimed part of its territory--Germany to the west, Austria and Hungary to the south and Poland to the north. Its relations with Poland, soured by the Teschen conflict, did not improve and it did not obtain a corridor linking it with Yugoslavia as it had demanded at the Peace Conference. The Peace Conference therefore failed to create a stable and durable system in the region. The collapse of Germany and the arrival of the Soviet Union on the scene after 1945 created a totally new situation and offered a new start.

Notes

1. On the early history of Slovakia, see S.J. Kirschbaum, *Slovaques et Tchèques: Essai sur Un Nouveau Aperçu de Leur Histoire Politique*, Lausanne: Collection Slavica, Editions l'Age de l'Homme, 1987, pp. 29-46.

2. See Robert A. Kann, *A History of the Habsburg Empire: 1526-1918,* Berkeley: University of California Press, 1974, pp. 25-45 and 70-77.

3. On early Slovak culture, see Kann, *A History of the Habsburg Empire*, pp. 389-90 and also R. Perréal and J.A. Mikuš, Lausanne, *La Slovaquie: Une Nation au Coeur de l'Europe*, L'Age de l'Homme, 1992, pp. 104-127.

4. See the Czech leader, František Palacky, to the Frankfurt Parliament of April 11, 1848, quoted in Kirschbaum, *Slovaques et Tchèques*, pp. 149-154.

5. Ibid., p. 96.

6. Ibid., pp. 97-99 and text in Appendix II, pp. 155-159.

7. On this, see K. Rebro "The Slovak question in the Revolutionary Years 1848-49" in Studia Historica Slovaca IV, 1966, p. 117. A Slovak National Council was established on September 16, 1848, and proclaimed Slovak independence from Hungary.

8. A.J.P. Taylor, *The Habsburg Monarchy*, Harmondsworth: Penguin Books, 1972, p. 81.

9. Kann, *A History of the Habsburg Empire*, pp. 318-326.

10. Ibid., pp. 320, 324.

11. Ibid., p. 328.

12. Kann, *A History of the Habsburg Empire*, pp. 329-330.

13. H. Andics, *Das Österreichische Jahrhundert: Die Donau - Monarchie 1804-1900,* Wien: Austriaca, 1984, pp. 99 and 167-8.

14. J.P. Bled, *François Joseph*, Paris, Fayard, 1987, p. 273.

15. Kann, *A History of the Habsburg Empire*, p. 275.

16. For the Ausgleich's terms and its consequences, see Kann, *A History of the Habsburg Empire*, pp. 333-338.

17. Ibid., p. 334.

18. On the proposed second Czech Ausgleich, see Kann, *A History of the Habsburg Empire*, pp. 358-360.

19. Cited in Kann, *A History of the Habsburg Empire*, at p. 339.

20. Ibid., p. 359.

21. On Czech politics in this period, see Kann, *A History of the Habsburg Empire*, pp. 349-350.

22. On the renewed effort at compromise, see Kann, *A History of the Habsburg Empire*, pp. 441-442.

23. A. Kann, "Karl Renner," *Journal of Modern History*, XXIII (1951), pp. 243-249 and Kann, *A History of the Habsburg Empire*, p. 442.

24. For developments in Slovakia, see Kirschbaum, *Slovaques et Tchèques*, pp. 106-112.

25. On the foundation of the Matica Slovenska, see J.A. Mikuš, "Slovakia: A Political and Constitutional History" in Slovak Studies, XXIV (1984), pp. 20-25.

26. Memorandum of the Slovak People to the Budapest Parliament, June 6-7, 1861, cited in Kirschbaum, *Slovaques et Tchèques*, Appendix III.

27. Kirschbaum, *Slovaques et Tchèques*, pp. 110-111.

28. Ibid., p. 110 and J. Lettrich, *A History of Modern Slovakia*, New York: Praeger, 1944, p. 44.

29. For the evolution of Allied thinking, see D. Stevenson, *The First World War and International Politics*, Oxford: Clarendon, 1991, pp. 216-221.

30. For early wartime Czechoslovak thinking, see D. Perman, *The Shaping of the Czechoslovak State*, Leiden, Brill: 1962, pp. 8-27.

31. On the separate peace negotiations, see F. Fejtö, *Requiem pour Un Empire Defunt: Histoire de la Destruction de l'Autriche-Hongrie*, Paris: Points, EDIMA, 1992, pp. 208-240.

32. See D. Perman, *The Shaping of the Czechoslovak State*, pp. 37-39, on recognition.

33. R. Perréal and J.A. Mikuš, *La Slovaquie: Une Nation au Coeur de l'Europe*, p. 66.

34. For discussion of these options and the Slovak movement in America and France, see Perréal and Mikuš, *La Slovaquie: Une Nation au Coeur de l'Europe*, pp. 44-48.

35. Cited in Kirschbaum, *Slovaques et Tchèques*, p. 170.

36. Cited ibid., p. 172.

37. Ibid., pp. 174-175.

38. For discussion of these different Czech viewpoints, see Perman, *The Shaping of the Czechoslovak State*, pp. 15-27 and Masaryk's map, endpiece.

39. Perman, *The Shaping of the Czechoslovak State*, p. 70 and pp. 123-125.

40. For French views, see ibid., pp. 131-138.

41. Ibid., p. 275.

42. Kirschbaum, *Slovaques et Tchèques*, pp. 120-122.

43. S. Grant-Cooper, *Europe and the Czechs*, Harmondsworth: Penguin Books, 1938, pp. 118-132, discusses the evolution of Sudeten German politics in Czechoslovakia.

44. H. Bodgan, *Histoire des Pays de l'Est*, Paris, Perrin: 1990, pp. 275-278.

45. On these plans, see Perréal and Mikuš, *La Slovaquie: Une Nation au Coeur de l'Europe*, pp. 51-52.

46. Ibid., p. 53.

47. Ibid., p. 54.

48. Ibid., p. 54.

49. Ibid., p. 56, footnote 1.

50. Ibid., pp. 56-57.

51. Ibid., pp. 57-60.

52. On the characterisation of the Slovak National Movemnet, see W. Laqueur, *Fascism*, New York: Penguin Books, 1979, pp. 237-239.

53. On the resistance and the Slovak National Rising (1946), see Kirschbaum, *Slovaques et Tchèques*, pp. 134-138 and M.R.D. Foot, *SOE: the Special Operations Executive - 1940-46*, London: BBC Publications, 1984, pp. 202-203.

54. On Beněs' policy, see Perréal and Mikuš, *La Slovaquie: Une Nation au Coeur de l'Europe*, pp. 61-65.

55. J. Rupnik, *The Other Europe*, London: Weidenfeld and Nicolson, 1988, pp. 87-92. A discussion between Beněs and Molotov is reported (88), in which Molotov says "I understand. You need Soviet help against the Slovaks." (December 1943).

56. Bogdan, *Histoire des Pays de l'Est*, p. 261.

57. On Hungarian foreign policy, see Bogdan, *Histoire des Pays de l'Est*, pp. 311-314.

58. Laqueur, *Fascism*, pp. 218-220 and pp. 231-237.

59. On Hungarian domestic politics between the wars, see Bogdan, *Histoire des Pays de l'Est*, pp. 282-285 and pp. 361-364.

3

The Communist Intermezzo

For forty years, the region was dominated by the communist system that was gradually established in the late 1940s. In theory, nationalist conflicts were banished. In reality, they were not resolved, but merely shelved to re-emerge after the fall of Communism in 1989. The communist regimes themselves were at times not above using nationalist issues, appropriating them to their own ends. As we shall see, especially in Czechoslovakia, much of the political debate that went on within the system--however much it was couched in communist ideological language--was often, in reality, a continuation by other means and in other forms of earlier nationalist conflicts. In one sense that might have been positive. The communist system imposed a rough and ready regional unity on the area for the first time since 1918. As part of the communist bloc, it was integrated into the COMECON economic system of socialist, international economic planning, directed in large measure from Moscow.

The establishment of a communism system and the Soviet model of industrialisation and planning created the conditions for the implementation of the Gabčikovo-Nagymaros project. Indeed, such a project was a typical product of Soviet-style economic planning. Gabčikovo-Nagymaros, with its vast scales, could hardly have been conceived and developed in any other political system. We therefore need to look at how Communism became established in the region and examine its principle characteristics.

Although western Czechoslovakia, including Plzen, was liberated by the Americans and Prague could have been, they tacitly accepted that Czechoslovakia was in the Soviet sphere.[1] Indeed, as we have seen, the Czechoslovak exile government itself recognised this fact as early as December 1943. As for Hungary, despite the 50:50 spheres of influence agreement between Churchill and Stalin in October 1944,[2] Hungary was entirely occupied by the Red Army and as an enemy country was subject to the tutelage of an Allied, in effect Soviet Armistice Commission until the Paris Peace Treaty of 1947. Thus, despite the formal difference in their status, the practical position of the two countries as key strategic links in the Soviet glacis in central Europe was very similar. They were also similar in terms of domestic political developments.

All over central Europe, the communist system was only gradually established between 1944-48. During this period, there was a degree of democratic space and some limited return to pre-war political circumstances with, of course, the elimination of the far right and everywhere an expanded role for the communist parties. The destruction of democracy, however limited, and the installation of the Stalinist system took the longest in Hungary and Czechoslovakia and the initial prospects for development of a moderately democratic political system were the brightest there.[3]

National circumstances and situations varied between the central European states, as did the exact pace of developments. However, a broad pattern unfolded everywhere in central Europe that began with broad democratic coalitions, then to communist control, then to purges within the communist party and imposition of the Stalinist system, with integration into a tight political, economic and military bloc directed in all essential policy matters from Moscow.[4] This process followed a number of distinct phases and, at decisive points, responded to specific Soviet direction. That said, it would be an over-simplification simply to regard these processes as part of a pre-ordained Soviet master plan that unfolded as laid down. It would be even more facile to regard those developments as part of a wider Soviet plan to control the whole of Europe. In reality, Stalin's policy was more cautious and opportunistic that it was adventurist. Certainly, like his Czarist predecessors, he was concerned to create a friendly glacis in central Europe. Hungary and Czechoslovakia had key strategic positions between the northern and southern tier and astride Soviet communications to their occupation zones in eastern Austria and Germany. But it should not be forgotten that Stalin still needed to be very cautious to avoid provoking a western reaction. He did no more, in his own eyes at least, than seek to consolidate the sphere he thought was accorded to him at Yalta. At the same time, in Greece, France and Italy for example, he respected western pre-eminence.[5] Only after late 1947, when it became clear that the division of Germany was imminent and that the moderate line in central Europe would produce no further dividends in relation to the west, did the Soviet Union consolidate its position in the region by liquidating the two last semi-democratic states, Czechoslovakia and Hungary, purging the local communist parties and integrating central and eastern Europe firmly into the Soviet-dominated bloc.[6]

In addition to these external factors, there were also important internal factors in post-war central Europe that favoured the communist cause. These ranged from the genuine desire for social reform, perceived abandonment by the west; and the discrediting of the old regime and through its real or manufactured links with collaboration. The non-communist parties acted almost as it they had accepted in advance their own demise before the progress of Communism as inevitable and, indeed, as the communists themselves maintained, in line with the march of history.

Thus, the main non-communist parties in each country, the Hungarian Smallholders' Party (SPP) and the Czechoslovak National Socialists (the party of Masaryk and Beneš) failed to develop any effective alternative strategy and accepted the fatal cooperation with the communists, even when, as in the case of Hungary, the SPP won an absolute majority of the 1945 elections. The old Social Democrats, with long-standing traditions in both countries, were unable to resist pressure for the otherwise desirable unification of the working class movement. Under the wider circumstances of central Europe in the late 1940s, this inevitably meant their submergence in a party that was apparently new, but in reality was the Communist Party under a new name.

In Hungary,[7] following the installation of the Fascist Arrow Cross government by the Germans in late 1944, a National Independence Front was set up in Szeged, uniting moderate figures of the Horthy period with smallholders, national peasants, socialists and communists. On December 21, the National Front established a provisional government in Debrecen under General Miklos de Donak. This government declared war on Germany but was nevertheless subject to the supervision of an Allied, but in reality essentially Soviet, Control Commission and the country remained occupied by Soviet troops.

The political parties proceeded to hold rapid elections to ensure the legitimacy of the regime as early as possible. However, only the four parties within the National Front were permitted to take part. The SPP won 57 percent of the vote and 246 seats, compared with 70 seats for the communists, 69 for the Socialists, 29 for the National Peasants and two others. The success of the SPP was mainly due to the fact that it was the most rightist of the authorized parties. Unfortunately, the communists had already infiltrated it with sympathetic elements.

The combination of Soviet pressure and indecision by the SPP leadership led to the formation of a National Front coalition, including communists as

Deputy Premier and Interior Minister under Mr. Tildy (SPP), rather than a one-party SPP government without the communists. Worse, the SPP tolerated and supported a radical purge and many death sentences against even moderate Horthyites and agreed to the institution of a Republic. Tildy became President and was replaced by Ferenc Nagy (SPP) as Premier.

Seeking to split the SPP, the communists made use of the usual tactics of constant synthetic public agitation and pressure and exploitation of economic problems and hyper-inflation. Acting as if in opposition though they were in government, the communists made accusations of collaboration, plots and sabotage "discovered" by the AVO (political police), who were controlled by the communist Interior Minister. In 1946, there were several expulsions of the SPP deputies. The anti-communist SPP leader, Bela Kovacs, was accused of implication in a plot and arrested. In May 1947, the Prime Minister also was accused of involvement in a plot and forced to resign and leave the country. The communists now considered that the time was ripe to force new elections. The National Front held together and in it, the communists with 21.8 percent (+4 percent only) became the largest party as the SPP collapsed to 17 percent. Cleverly, a non-National Front opposition (six parties) was allowed at the election, which split the anti-communist vote. The National Front obtained 60.2 percent of the vote and 269 seats. The opposition parties won 39.8 percent and 142 seats. Now, pressure was stepped up on the socialists, as the SPP had already been reduced to docile impotence. The right and centre in the Socialist Party were accused of fresh plots and expelled by the weak leadership. This led, in June 1948, to the fusion of the communists and socialists in the Hungarian Socialist Workers' Party under the communist Matyas Rakosi. The SPP President of the Republic was also eliminated by false accusations, opening the way to full Stalinisation.

As we have seen, the Czechoslovak leadership sought to reach any early compromise with the Soviet Union and orientate Czech post-war policy towards cooperation with the USSR.[8] This meant a domestic alliance between the communists and non-communists, a policy of social reform, expulsion of the three million Sudeten Germans and reimposition of Czech centralism. All these policies received the approval of Moscow. Thus, a coalition cabinet was formed under the socialist Ždenek Fierlinger composed of communists (eight ministers), Socialists, National Socialists and other resistance leaders in the liberated city of Košiče in April 1945. It issued a radical socio-economic programme involving wide-ranging nationalisations of companies with over 500 employees and agrarian reform. It was also agreed that there would be elections in early 1946 and that the largest party would lead the government, though all the National Front parties would remain in coalition.[9] This coalition proceeded to expel all but a minority of clearly anti-Nazi Sudeten Germans, as agreed with the Allies. At the same time, measures were taken against the Hungarian minority, which among other things led to the expulsion of close to 180,000, either by deportation, population exchange with Slovaks from Hungary or forced resettlement outside the areas of Hungarian settlement.[10] With the expulsion of the Germans, extermination of its Jewish population by the Nazis and the measures against the Hungarian minority, the restored Czechoslovakia became much more ethnically homogeneous. Hungary, as an Axis state, was forced to return the areas obtained by the Vienna award and ceded three further villages on the southern bank of the Danube near Bratislava in the Paris Peace Treaty of 1947. These villages were subsequently important to Slovakia in implementing the unilateral diversion of the Danube in 1992.

The 1946 election--the fairest in central Europe--saw strong communist support, which reflected the traditional left-wing strength in Bohemia. The communists (KŠC) took 38 percent in the country as a whole, though only about 30 percent in Slovakia. The KŠC won 114 seats in the 300-seat Assembly. With the socialists, 13 percent and 37 seats, the left won a narrow overall majority (151 seats). The three permitted non-socialist parties within the National Front won 49 percent. The National Socialists (more nationally minded and more centrist than the socialists) won 18 percent, the People's Party won 16 percent and the Democrats (a Slovak party) won 15 percent.[11] The prior agreement to appoint the Prime Minister from the strongest party, to maintain the National Front and the openness to a fusion between the KŠC and socialists manifested by the left-wing faction of the socialists placed the communists in a very strong position, even though three-fifths of voters did not vote for them.

The communists had another advantage as the only broad-based national party. The KŠC, Socialists, National Socialists and the People's Party were traditional parties that had existed before the war. The pre-war Slovak parties were dissolved as collaborationist. The Democratic Party emerged from the Slovak resistance and included many Protestants, whereas the pre-war nationalists were mainly Catholics. The People's Party was also a Christian party in the Czech lands. Thus, the Democratic Party was exclusively Slovak; the People's Party, National Socialists and Socialists were almost exclusively Czech.[12]

The new Cabinet was, as before, a coalition of the Popular Front parties under the leadership of Klement Gottwald (KŠC) as Prime Minister. The communists held 9 of the 25 ministries, including Interior (although not the Justice Ministry), Finance, Information, Agriculture (patronage in the rural repopulated Sudeten areas), and Foreign Trade. The key economic portfolio of Industry Minister was held by a socialist.[13] The KŠC also achieved control over the trade union federation.[14] The Defense Minister, General Svoboda, was not a declared communist, but was sufficiently close to the party to guarantee them the neutrality of the armed forces, which were thus not available to the non-communist forces in the crisis of February 1948.[15]

The communists increased pressure on several fronts at once. They mobilised opinion in favour of radical economic reforms. They sought control in Slovakia, which was effectively reduced to a colony as its indigenous political forces were discredited through their support for the Slovak Republic. Formally, there was some improvement in the constitutional situation of Slovakia within the Czechoslovakian state.[16] After the aborted reforms of 1939 and the interlude of the independent Slovak republic, it was difficult if not impossible to return to a purely unitary state, so Slovakia was given a special status with its own National Council and Council of Commissioners (government). Despite this apparent devolution, the reality was soon to become even more centralistic than in the past. In 1945 and 1946, three agreements were adopted that reduced this already limited autonomy. Furthermore, despite the weakness of the KŠC in Slovakia, Gustav Husak, Slovak communist leader, became the Chairman of the Council of Commissioners. To keep up the pressure, Monsignor Tiso, the President of the wartime Slovak Republic, and Prime Minister Tuka were executed, despite requests for clemency from the whole Slovak political spectrum.

The communists moved to split and discredit all their most dangerous rivals, in turn. They began with the majority party in Slovakia, the Democrats, then turned to the National Socialists and the Socialists, who were to be pressured into a merger with the KŠC and President Beneš and Foreign Minister Jan Masaryk, son of the state's first President. Husak accused the Democrats (of a nationalist conspiracy), especially its leader Joseph Littrich and Democrat Deputy Ursiny. The KŠC mobilised mass demonstrations in Bratislava and sought to impose purges on the Democrats and broaden the Slovak National Front to include representatives of the trade unions and other social organisations that were under effective communist control. These tactics were too brutal and premature. They backfired badly as the Socialist Congress then meeting in Brno rejected merger and elected an anti-merger leader, Bohumil Lanšman, to replace Zdenek Fierlinger, a strong supporter of the merger. Gottwald backed down and proposed a compromise that was a defeat for the KŠC in the short term, but still left the Democrats weakened.[17]

The Czechoslovak cabinet at first accepted participation in the Marshall Plan in July 1947, but Gottwald insisted on submitting the matter to Moscow. The Soviet leadership forced the Czechoslovak government (and the Polish government) to retreat. It was a severe blow for Beneš and Masaryk. It showed the very narrow margin for manoeuvre both for Czech policy and for the non-communist parties.[18]

In September 1947 at the COMINFORM Summit, KŠC General Secretary Slansky had been criticised for the slow rate of progress in Czechoslovakia and exhorted to accelerate the move into what Seton-Watson called the final phase. Slansky responded, significantly, that the KŠC would move to the offensive domestically, as it had internationally, referring no doubt to the Marshall Plan incident. He said that the KŠC would move to "unmask reactionary elements and eliminate them from the National Front parties."[19] As it exactly fit this approach, very likely the Slovak crisis in November was a testing of the waters.

By early 1948, with the relative failures at both Bratislava and Brno, there was something of a stand-off. The non-communists now realised that a passive approach would lead to them to being undermined by salami tactics. They had to act. The area they targetted--the police and security services--was well chosen. Indeed, they did need to rein in the communist-controlled apparatus of destabilisation. However, their approach was ill-thought out, ill-prepared and amateurish. Above all, it underestimated the communists and ignored the ground lost by the non-communists since 1945. The non-communist parties that provoked the crisis failed to ensure in advance the solid support of the socialists, of Masaryk as an independent with universal prestige and, above all, of President Beneš. They did not mobilise public opinion, nor even their party activists. They acted as if they were involved in a routine pre-war musical chairs cabinet crisis.[20]

In February 1948, they demanded that the KŠC Interior Minister Nosek reinstate non-communist police officials and put an end to political appointments in the police. Clearly, the communists were unlikely to comply and probably were not expected to do so. The liberals (National Socialists and People's Party) wanted a confrontation. All non-communist ministers supported their demands, but when these were not met, only 12 (NS and People's Party) ministers--a minority--actually resigned. Gottwald was not therefore legally obliged to hand in the resignation of the cabinet as a whole, opening the way for elections as the non-communists' script had it. Now, the liberals were on the defensive and the ball was in the court of President Beneš. The liberals were obliged to backpedal, and hope he would reject their resignations! The communists mobilised street pressure, but it was barely needed. President Beneš capitulated. The government was reconstructed with tighter communist control, but included a few dissident populists and National Socialists who were part of the destabilisation process. Now, elections could take place on May 30 but under totally different circumstances. There was no opposition to the National Front and soon the socialists finally merged with the communists.[21]

In both countries, the final communist takeover saw intensification of both the subversion of any remaining groups not yet under communist control and more unbridled application of police terror to create a monolithic Stalinist system of total party control. The leaders of the Czech National Socialist Party were tried and several were executed, including Milada Horakova. In all, over 7,000 National Socialists were tried in 1950. Between 1948 and 1954, there were close to 150,000 political prisoners in Czechoslovakia. 77,000 Czech intellectuals were sacked from their posts in 1951. In Hungary, 700,000 people were sentenced between 1948 and 1953. For 1952 alone, the figure was 144,743.[22]

The second phase was to bring the communist parties themselves under tight Stalinist control, through a system of terror, denunciation and purges similar to that employed in the Soviet Union in the 1930s.[23] As it was, the communist parties had in their short period of ostensibly open democratic activity expanded greatly and taken in large sections of the local resistance and intelligentsia. In almost all of the parties--certainly in the Czech and Hungarian--there was a division between the "Muscovites," who spent the war or longer periods of exile in the USSR and re-emerged in the baggage train of the Red Army such as the KŠC leader Gottwald and HSWP leader Matyas Rakosi, and the "natives" from the local underground resistance who had also been in the west or the International Brigades in Spain. The "Muscovites" were much more closely under the control of the international department of the NKVD (secret police) and of the Soviet Party's Central Committee that replaced the COMINTERN when the latter was dissolved in 1943.

During the Titoist purge period lasting from 1948 until Stalin's death, there were drastic reductions in the number of party members, with one in four being weeded out. The next and more grotesque stage was the purge in the upper echelons of parties, including those who, such as Slansky in Czechoslovakia or Rajk in Hungary, had just played a key role in brutally crushing non-communist opposition. The revolution ate its children with a vengeance. The purges and show trials were most vicious in Prague and Budapest, perhaps because the parties there had the longest normal political existence. A disgusting aspect of these trials was the crude revival of anti-Semitism.[24] Far from the old Czech-Slovak problem being resolved by the communist take-over, it now was played out in these internecine struggles within the Czechoslovak Communist Party. The Slovak communist and Czechoslovak Foreign Minister Clementis was accused of being a "National Communist" and executed. In almost the last Stalinist purge, the Slovak Ivan Horvath was convicted of bourgeois nationalism as part of centralising pressure.[25]

The death of Stalin on March 5, 1953, did not immediately lead to liberalisation in central and eastern Europe. Indeed, the Party leadership in the satellite countries did not know how to read the first tentative signals coming from Moscow from the new post-Stalin collective leadership, especially after the liquidation of Beria, head of the security services. There were soon some limited signs of détente: the Korean War came to an end in late 1953, the Geneva Agreements in 1954 brought an end to the Indo-Chinese War. In Europe, the Austrian state treaty was signed and Soviet troops left Austria in October 1955. Soviet troops left Finland in the same year. There was little immediate impact in central Europe itself, though there was a slackening in the trials and repression. Some of the first-generation communist leaders such as Gottwald and Rakosi left the scene.

It was, though, the 20th Congress of the CPSU in February 1956, at which Khrushchev launched his denunciation of Stalin's crimes and cult of personality, that sent tremours through the whole of central and eastern Europe.[26] The rumours about the secret speech and indeed versions of it spread like wildfire within the Soviet bloc. The shock waves were significant, especially in Poland and Hungary, though not in Czechoslovakia, where there were no changes in the leadership in 1956. Thus, Antonin Zapotocky, the trade union leader of 1948, succeeded Gottwald from 1953 to 1957 and on his death was succeeded in his turn undramatically by Antonin Novotny. Indeed, the Czechoslovak response to the dramatic events of 1956 was a tightening up that, as we shall see, led to the adoption of the new "socialist" and even more centralist Constitution in 1960.[27]

It was in Hungary and Poland that the events of the 1953-1956 period, culminating in the 20th Congress, had the deepest effect. The Austrian state treaty, neutralisation of Austria and the withdrawal of Soviet troops made a deep impact in neighbouring Hungary. That event showed that the Soviets could be persuaded to withdraw and deprived them of any argument for a continued military presence in Hungary, even though the newly founded Warsaw Pact of 1955 provided a basis for continued military cooperation and integration.

The Hungarian leadership was weak and indecisive in its reaction to destalinisation. Rakosi was relegated to part of a three-man collective leadership in late 1953. There was timid liberalisation and some prisoners were freed. However, the Rakosiyte old guard struck back and removed the reformist Premier Imre Nagy, but it was difficult to put back the clock. There was a new spirit among the peasants, among students, intellectuals in the Petöfi Circle and non-communist former political leaders from the 1945-1947 period such as Bela Kovacs and Zoltan Tildy. There was a rising chorus of criticism and open demands to reinstate Nagy. Inside the party, too, these pressures were felt, crystallising around the issue of the rehabilitation of the executed former leader, Lazlo Rajk. On October 6, 1956, he was rehabilitated before a crowd of 150,000. These measures and the final removal of Rakosi as Party Secretary and his replacement by a Rakosi supporter, Ernest Gerö, was far too little too late.

Students in Szeged, Debrecen and Budapest organised independent student associations and launched a 14-point manifesto demanding the withdrawal of Soviet forces and the return to power of Imre Nagy. On October 23, the Budapest students organised a banned demonstration in support of the Polish Reform Movement at the Statue of General Bem, a Polish general who had led Hungarian forces during the 1848 revolution. Workers joined in the demonstration. There was a revolutionary atmosphere and the political police fired on the crowd. Provocative speeches by Gerö against "enemies of socialism" were met with violence against symbols of the regime, such as the hated statue of Stalin. Imre Nagy was recalled as Prime Minister on October 24, 1956.

The situation was explosive and the new leadership's timid steps and appeals for calm did nothing to reduce tension. Indeed, there was a very real threat of Soviet intervention on the basis of a request from the former leadership. It seems that there was a genuine reluctance on the part of the Soviet leadership, itself strongly divided, to go down that route at that stage. As a result, there was only a very limited increase in the Soviet military presence and no intervention directed against the new government. Indeed, the Soviets themselves negotiated a change in the party leadership from the discredited Gerö to Kadar. In essence, the Soviet leadership seemed to prefer to allow the new Kadar/Nagy government some time to master the situation.

In view of that apparent green light from Moscow and faced with growing and uncontrollable pressures from society, the government felt able to follow its own reformist instincts and put itself boldly at the head of the reform movements.[28]

Thus, the government proposed measures more radical than either the Dubček leadership during the Prague Spring or even the first Solidarnosc cabinet in Poland in 1909. Political pluralism, free elections, neutrality and withdrawal from the Warsaw Pact were on the agenda. With hindsight, this was clearly "a bridge too far," which went beyond any possible consensus within the ruling party and clearly represented a dangerous provocation for the Soviet Union. It is indeed hard to see how the Soviet leadership could have ignored these developments. Had it done so, there would have been inevitable chain reactions in Poland and possibly in the GDR and Czechoslovakia.

Unlike the situation thirty years later, the world climate was unfavourable, as the simultaneous Anglo-French intervention at the Suez Canal distracted western attention and seriously undermined western moral authority, especially in the neutralist Third World and even on the left in western Europe. There was a tendency to regard both actions as morally equivalent. Naturally, the United Nations could not act against Soviet intervention, as the Security Council would be paralysed by a Soviet veto.

Equally, the internal situation was fundamentally different. Despite the uncertainties of destalinisation, the Hungarian Party retained levels of power and a reserve of self-confidence that had evaporated by 1988. Thus, Janos Kadar, a "realist," established an alternative "counter" government of workers and peasants on November 4, 1956, that could, with Soviet support, credibly form the basis of a new post-uprising regime.

Thus, after an apparent withdrawal, Soviet troops returned to Hungary on October 31 after a very difficult debate about intervention in the Politburo and Central Committee of the Soviet Party. The final decision in favour of intervention was undoubtedly only made possible because of the decision of the Hungarian government to leave the Warsaw Pact, announced on October 31, and under the "cover" of the Suez crisis which reduced the foreign policy cost of intervention to the USSR. After bloody fighting between supporters of the Nagy government and Soviet forces, especially in Budapest, Cspel (an industrial town near Budapest) and Györ on the Moson Danube near the Austrian border, the uprising was defeated by November 13. The consequences were tragic: Thousands were killed in the fighting; some 350-400, including Imre Nagy and Pal Maleter, his Defence Minister, were executed and up to 22,000 more were imprisoned. Some 220,000 Hungarians went into exile.[29]

In the longer term, the consequences of the failure of the uprising were less negative and more paradoxical than it appeared at first sight. Certainly, in the immediate aftermath of the uprising, repression was severe. Thereafter, a gradual thaw set in, leading to considerable economic reform, though without significant political reform, coupled with a degree of mutual tolerance between the regime and its opponents. Both sides in effect were learning the invisible limits that neither could cross. The people could not expect to remove the regime as long as the geopolitical situation remained unchanged, and the regime could not expect the positive loyalty of any but a small minority of the population. This gave rise to the notion of "goulash Communism," of Hungary as the "happiest hut in the socialist camp." It also gave rise to Kadar's telling redefinition of the leading role of the party in his famous formula "Who is not against us is with us." While not condoning opposition, this formula recognised its existence. This was a gradual and complex process that involved combining liberalisation internally with reassurances for the USSR in the form of full acceptance of COMECON integration, which began in earnest after 1956 and was intensified with the adoption in June 1962 of the "Fundamental Principles of International Socialist Division of Labour."[30]

Internally, the worst repression ended in 1959 and the regime began to prepare for an economic reform that could be combined with a degree of cultural liberalisation and some opening of borders, enabling Hungarians to travel abroad, but without political liberalisation. After a few years of intensive preparation, the New Economic Mechanism was introduced in 1968.[31] The reforms gave greater freedom to a small sector of private enterprise (the parallel economy) on the periphery of the state economy, especially in the service sector and in agriculture. These sectors were also able to resolve some of the most severe deficiencies of the state sector, providing a safety valve. At the core of the state economy, deregulation was limited and subsidies remained. More realistic exchange rates and heavy borrowing from the west maintained a high rate of economic growth, increasing real incomes and rising consumption. Hungarians also were allowed to travel abroad in large numbers. The economy grew: 5.8 percent from 1951-1960, 4.1 percent from 1961-1965 and an excellent 6.6 percent in the 1966-1975 period.[32]

However, by the 1980s, these limited reforms had run their course and could no longer energise the economy, as structural reforms had been avoided. Certainly, almost 400,000 people worked in the private sector and in 1986, a bankruptcy law was enacted, but the private sector was still an inadequate critical mass and was beset by regulations, intervention and non-application of market principles elsewhere in the system. With the onset of the economic crisis, indebtedness rose dramatically to $17.6 billion by 1988, the record debt per head in central Europe. Growth fell back to below 1 percent by 1988. Inflation reached almost 20 percent in 1986 and 25 percent in 1988. Concealed unemployment became a serious problem. Income tax and value added tax (VAT) were introduced to cover the increasing subsidies for non-profit-making state enterprises. It became clear that a more radical approach, which could no longer exclude political reforms, would be needed.[33]

Czechoslovakia, on the other hand, remained quiescent throughout the 1950s. Even the Hungarian minority in Slovakia was apparently unaffected by the 1956 Hungarian uprising. But in 1986, the next testing of the limits to reform within the Soviet bloc came in Czechoslovakia with the Prague Spring, ending once again with Soviet military intervention. This time, Hungary did not move. Indeed, worse, Hungarian forces took part in the Warsaw Pact invasion of their neighbour in August 1968.

On the surface, the issue was simple: reform against reaction. Yet, the reality was a good deal more complex. As ever, the Prague Reform Movement was also linked into the perennial Czech/Slovak conflict. An alliance of Czech reformers and Slovak Nationalists and Conservatives brought Alexander Dubček, a Slovak, to power as General Secretary of the Czechoslovak Communist Party in January 1968.

This launched the Prague Spring, whose roots lay in the earlier Slovak liberalisation. Even as seen from a Soviet perspective, dangerous as it might be, the Prague Spring was certainly far from the "counter-revolution" of Budapest in 1956. In many ways, it was an internal matter. In 1960, the Socialist Constitution virtually revoked the limited autonomy won by Slovakia in 1945. The repression of Slovakia intensified. Slovak intellectuals rallied around the cultural magazine Kulturny Život against the arbitrary Czech-dominated system. The issue of the rehabilitation of Clementis, Husak and other Slovaks and Novotny's maladroit attacks on both Slovak communists and the Slovak cultural institution, Matica Slovenska, sharpened the existing tensions between the Czechs and Slovaks.[34] As Dubček, Regional Party Secretary in Bratislava at this point put it, "The Slovak Party was substantially subordinated to the Czech one"[35] and, referring to the 1960 Constitution, "these measures significantly increased centralisation in Prague and showing arrogant disregard for Slovak interests and feelings, ignored the bitter lessons of the First Czechoslovak Republic in the 1930s."[36] Taking up the battle against Novotny's anti-Slovak policies, he came into open conflict with Novotny on rehabilitation and economic policy towards Slovakia. He built alliances with other Slovaks, with Czech reformers and even anti-Novotny conservatives, winning control of the Slovak Party from its previous pro-Czech controllers on his election as Slovak Party Secretary in 1963. From that position, he protected the activities of the intellectuals around Kulturny Život. Slovakia suddenly became much more liberal than Prague and pushed for much more rapid destalinisation.[37]

With Khrushchev's distant benign support, Dubček survived Novotny's efforts to remove him as conflict escalated over Dubček's support for economic market reforms and a degree of political liberalisation. In the event, by 1968, Dubček was able to himself challenge and overturn Novotny. Thus, in January 1968, left without Soviet support, Novotny finally was forced to resign and Dubček was elected First Secretary of the Czechoslovak Party by a coalition of Slovaks, Moravian regionalists from Ostrova and Czech reformers.

With Novotny's removal from the First Secretaryship and then in March from the Presidency, what was in essence a negative coalition lost its cement. The Dubček leadership contained several loose and divergent factions: radical reformers (e.g., Kriegel, Smrkovsky), moderate reformers (Dubček, Černik, the Prime Minister), anti-reformers (Kolder, Indra, Bilak, Jakeš, later First Secretary after Husak) and a swing middle group. Some of the anti-reformists such as Kolder and Bilak had, though, been activist members of the anti-Novotny coalition.[38] As Soviet and other Warsaw Pact criticism strengthened and as preparations for the Party Congress (initially planned for the autumn of 1968) advanced both nationally and in Slovakia, it became obvious that there would be a major clear-out. The leadership polarised.[39] These internal dissensions slowed up the formulation of a reform agenda and watered it down when finally, on April 5, 1968, the Action Programme was adopted by the Central Committee. As Dubček himself put it, reflecting in his memoirs on the criticisms that he either went too fast or too slow,

> Even looking back after almost 25 years, I do not see what I could or should have done otherwise...on every day of these short eight months I had to weigh carefully all the conflicting moves in play around me and prepare my next move accordingly. Furthermore, even after 5 January 1968, I had no reform-minded majority behind me in the expanded presidium or in the Central Committee. The make-up of the coalition that had ousted Novotny from the secretaryship was much more complex than that. Many of those who had

supported removing Novotny were not prepared for further steps towards reform, as I was well aware.[40]

As it was, the Action Programme, and even the far more critical and radical Two Thousand Words Manifesto launched in May by liberal intellectuals, remained relatively moderate. Even so, the Manifesto was seen by the leadership as dangerous. It was even criticised by the leadership's most noted liberal, Jozef Smrkovsky, the President of the National Assembly, as "political romanticism". Foreign Minister Hayek argued that the Manifesto gave aid and comfort to hardliners and the Soviet leadership by providing them with arguments against the Czechoslovak leadership.[41]

There was no commitment to political pluralism. The Social Democrats were "dissuaded" from refounding their party. Nor was the leading role of the KŠC or the foreign policy orientation of Czechoslovakia in any way changed. The Soviet leadership and the more hardline Warsaw Pact countries remained sceptical that the Czech leadership could hold to its commitments or keep the lid on the situation in the face of the re-emergence of an autonomous civil society that not only supported the reform programme, but sought to accelerate and deepen it. Indeed, this was perhaps the crux of the disagreement between Dubček and Brezhnev. For the Czechoslovaks, reform and the re-emergence of public opinion would strengthen the party and legitimise its leading role. For Brezhnev, such thinking was naive and dangerous.

There was, through the Dresden, Warsaw, Geneva and Bratislava meetings, a dialogue of the deaf, which eventually led to a decision to intervene militarily, although that decision was taken only reluctantly and with difficulty. Brezhnev himself was a reluctant intervener, preferring a political solution, but eventually came round to the view that intervention was necessary, building a coalition for the move within the divided Soviet Politburo. Timing was important. Intervention had to pre-empt the Czechoslovak Party Congress and take place before the World Communist Congress, where there would be support for the Prague Spring from western communist parties and before the climax of the American election campaign, both due in November. So, if it were done, it were well done quickly.[42]

The pro-interventionist coalition brought together many diverse strands: the ideologists: most of the security community--KGB and army; non-Russian, western USSR party leaders such as the Balts and, above all, Shelest from the Ukraine; and the harder-line Warsaw Pact leaders (Ulbricht from the GDR, Gomulka from Poland and Zhivkov from Bulgaria). Those concerned with foreign policy fallout and relations with the world communist movement were on the whole non-interventionist, as was the Hungarian leader, Janos Kadar, who sought to mediate between Prague and Moscow.

The issues at stake related to national security, but more centrally, to the dangers of igniting centrifugal political and nationalist forces within the Soviet bloc. Thus, logically, Shelest (the western Ukraine had been part of Czechoslovakia before 1945), Ulbricht, Gomulka and the Baltic communists feared the Prague Spring as did the Soviet ideologists, because its ideas could spread and fuse with nationalism. It should not be forgotten that the reform process had in part been ignited because of the Slovak issue.[43] Shelest and Gomulka were strongly insistent on this danger.

In the normalisation that followed the intervention, repression fell more heavily on the Czech lands and Slovakia. 500,000 members were expelled from the party, mostly Czechs. The normalisation was slower and more gradual than in Hungary. Dubček remained First Secretary until April 1969.[44] Slovakia was able to retain its one key gain from the Prague Spring: federalisation set out in the Action Programme and enacted in October 1968. The Slovak National Council and the Slovak government obtained important domestic competences. At the federal level, a two-Chamber Parliament with a Chamber of States with 75 Czech and 75 Slovak members flanked the National Assembly with co-equal legislative powers. The Slovak Husak succeeded Dubček and eventually, in 1975, also succeeded General Svoboda as President. He was the first Slovak to hold that office. The expansion of the military-industrial complex linked to the export of arms to the other Warsaw Pact and third world countries came to be mainly located in more politically reliable Slovakia. The key Soviet gas pipeline was also built through Slovakia. The post-1968 opposition to "normalisation" located among Prague intellectuals and in Charter 77 was a largely Czech phenomenon and was little echoed in Slovakia.

Communism had not abolished national sentiment and conflicts. Certainly, differences between Czechs and Slovaks had not disappeared. Slovaks still felt themselves to be unequally treated. Czechs regarded the Slovaks as collaborators with normalisation. The same was true in Hungary, where from the early 1980s the Hungarian communist authorities played the nationalist card in support of the Hungarian minorities, especially in Romania, but also in Slovakia and Voivodina. In Slovakia, there were arrests of Hungarian intellectuals in 1982 and facilities for the Hungarian minority were reduced.

The events of 1956 and 1968 were a major lesson in the limits of various types of reform movements. Thereafter, as we shall see in the next chapter, those who opposed communist hegemony adopted very different strategies from those of the Hungarian uprising and the Prague Spring. Yet, with hindsight, the uprising and the Prague Spring were important stages in the process of the collapse or implosion of Communism in 1989. They were, in a word, Rakosi's salami tactics in reverse. Yet, it was in precisely this long technocratic twilight, with mounting economic pressures for economic reform without political reforms that the key decisions about the Gabčikovo-Nagymaros project could be forced through.

Notes

1. Jan Rupnik, *The Other Europe*, London: Weidenfeld and Nicolson, 1988, pp. 70-71. Referring to the appeals of the Prague Insurgents for U.S. help in May 1945, Rupnik says "Eisenhower instructed Patton to observe the "spheres of liberation" agreed with the Russians."

2. Robin Edmonds, *The Big Three: Churchill, Roosevelt and Stalin in Peace and War*, Harmondsworth: Penguin, 1992, pp. 388-9.

3. Henry Bogdan, *Histoire des Pays de l'Est*, Paris: Perrin, 1990, categorises (400) these two countries as subject to the "progressive method."

4. Hugh Seton-Watson distinguishes three phases: genuine coalition, bogus coalition, monolithic communist control. See Seton-Watson, *From Lenin to Khrushchev: The History of World Communism*, Boulder: Westview, 1986. Rupnik refines in *The Other Europe* this into ten "common ingredients."

5. On Stalin's approach, see Alan Bullock, *Hitler and Stalin: Parallel Lives*, London: HarperCollins, 1991, pp. 984-1035, especially pp. 1011-1026.

6. A decision in this respect was taken at the COMINFORM conference of Skzlarzka Poreba (Poland) in September 1947. Rupik, *The Other Europe*, p 97.

7. On Hungary, see Bogdan, *Histoire des Pays de l'Est*, pp. 412-418 and Rupnik, *The Other Europe*, pp. 75-77.

8. Sources for the communist takeover in Czechoslovakia include Bogdan, *Histoire des Pays de l'Est*, pp. 419-424; Rupnik, *The Other Europe*, pp. 87-108 and Jean-Pierre Rageau, *Prague 148: le Rideau de Fer s'est Abattu,* Paris: Editions Complex, 1981. Rageau gives a detailed blow-by-blow account, pp. 41-59.

9. Nikolaus Von Preradovich, *Die Tschechoslowakei 1918-1992: Der Staat, den nur die Tschechen Wollten*, Starnberger, VGB: 1993, pp. 152-173.

10. *From Minority Status to Partnership: Hungarians in Czechoslovakia/Slovakia*, Bratislava: Political Movement Együtteles (coexistence): 1993, pp. 4-5.

11. Election results, Bogdan, *Histoire des Pays de l'Est*, pp. 419-421.

12. On the parties, see Bogdan, *Histoire des Pays de l'Est*, pp. 21-23.

13. Bogdan, *Histoire des Pays de l'Est*, p. 420.

14. Ibid., pp. 49-50.

15. Rupnik, *The Other Europe*, p. 99, quotes General Svoboda's statement on this to the KŠC Central Committee in September 1969.

16. On Slovak constitutional arrangements, see S. J. Kirschbaum, *Slovaques et Tchèques*, Seve Slavica, Age de l'Homme, 1987, pp. 142-3.

17. On this crisis, see F. Vnuk, "Slovak-Czech Relations 1945-1948" in ed. Kirschbaum S.J., *Slovak Politics: Essays on Slovak History in Honour of Joseph M. Kirschbaum*, Cleveland: Slovak Institute, pp. 314-371.

18. Rupnik, *The Other Europe*, pp. 95-96. He quotes Foreign Minister Masaryk as saying, "I left Moscow as Foreign Minister of a sovereign country, I returned as Stalin's vassal."

19. Rupnik, *The Other Europe*, p. 97.

20. On the strategic weakness of the liberal non-communists, see Rupnik, *The Other Europe*, 99. 98-101 and Rageau, *Prague 148: le Rideau de Fer s'est Abbatu*, pp. 91-92.

21. See chronology February 13, 1948, Rageau, *Prague 148: le Rideau de Fer s'est Abbatu*, pp. 41-59.

22. See Rupnik, *The Other Europe*, pp. 111-114 for statistics on the purges.

23. See Rupnik, *The Other Europe*, for the internal party purges, pp. 115-128 and G. Schöpflin, *Politics in Eastern Europe*, Oxford: Blackwell, 1993, pp. 75-80.

24. Rupnik, *The Other Europe*, pp. 122-3.

25. Bogdan, *Histoire des Pays de l'Est*, p. 444.

26. Ibid., pp. 450-452 for the early destalinisation and pp. 458-460 on the 20th Congress.

27. Kirschbaum, *Slovaques et Tchèques*, pp. 70-71 shows how the Prague leadership hesitated to destalinise as this would have involved reviving the Czech/Slovak conflict by rehabilitating the purged Slovaks.

28. For the events of the uprising, Bogdan, *Histoire des Pays de l'Est*, pp. 463-472.

29. J. Rainer, "The Reprisals" in New Hungarian Quarterly, 1993, pp. 118-127.

30. Bogdan, *Histoire des Pays de l'Est*, pp. 473-474 on COMECON.

31. J. Kornai, "The Hungarian Reform Process: Visions, Hope and Reality," Journal of Economic Literature, December, 1986.

32. G. Schöpflin *Politics in Eastern Europe*, Oxford: Blackwell, 1993, p. 130.

33. Bogdan, *Histoire des Pays de l'Est*, p. 558.

34. Kirschbaum, *Slovaques et Tchèques*, p. 143 on the tightening up.

35. Aleksander Dubček, *Hope Dies Last*, London: HarperCollins, 1993, p. 79.

36. Ibid., p. 81.

37. Dubček, passim., pp. 78-95.

38. Jiri Valenta, *Soviet Intervention in Czechoslovakia - 1968: Anatomy of a Decision*, Baltimore and London: John Hopkins University Press, 1991, p. 37.

39. Ibid., p. 42.

40. Dubček, *Hope Dies Last*, p. 128.

41. On the 2000 Word Manifesto, see Bogdan, *Histoire des Pays de l'Est*, p. 489, which also quotes Smrykovsky.

42. For an account of the events of the Prague Spring, see G. Skilling *Czechoslovakia's Interrupted Revolution*, Princeton: , Princeton University Press: 1976.

43. On the coalition politics in the Politburo, see Valenta, *Soviet Intervention in Czechoslovakia - 1968*.

44. Dubček, *Hope Dies Last*, pp. 240-241.

4

Towards Democracy

Everyone asks the question: How could communism, which seemed so monolithic and entrenched, just collapse without serious resistance? One possible explanation would be that the system had been dramatically eroded and eaten away from within, leaving a shell that collapsed when the external prop of the Brezhnev doctrine was removed by Gorbachev. The Emperor was naked, but until 1989 no one dared to say so far fear of provoking a Soviet reaction. As a result, the strategy of perestroika, namely what the moderate Czech reformers had hoped for, a genuine transformation that would legitimise the continuing rule of the party, became impossible. It was too little, too late. The communist party reformers were by then fighting a lost war.

Much of this evolution was subterranean. It was not easily visible behind the unchanging facade of communist power. Indeed, this low-key, patchy, barely visible development was inherent in the new post-1968 generation of activists all over central Europe and certainly in Hungary and Czechoslovakia. They drew important lessons from the failures of 1956 and 1968. By 1968, the Polish and Hungarian reformers of 1956, Gomulka and Kadar, had joined the Conservative camp. The Soviet responses in 1956 and 1968 showed that neither direct counter-revolutionary confrontation as in 1956 nor transformation of the party from above and below in a "push-pull" strategy, making it the vehicle for change, as in the Prague Spring, had any short- or long-term prospects of success. Neither the strategies of Imre Nagy nor Dubček, nor the longer-term ones of Gomulka/Kadar had led to sustainable reform. The parties could be neither removed nor reformed. Could they though simply be ignored and increasingly replaced by civil society in growing areas of private, social and even economic life, leaving only their monopoly in the political and international spheres intact?

Could the power of the party be made largely irrelevant or could the party be obliged by these developments to negotiate with society to create such reserved spheres?

These ideas, evolved by both intellectuals and practical activists in Poland, Hungary and Czechoslovakia did not arise in a vacuum. On the one hand, they were a response to the failures of 1956 and 1968. On the other hand, these events themselves had created openings. Central Europe was no longer as closed as it had been before 1956. Wider economic and political developments created new conditions. The lessons of 1956 and 1968 were that the party could neither be defeated nor transformed. However, the parties too, if only implicitly, had been forced to learn some lessons. These lessons were most clearly understood in Kadar's famous aphorism, "Those who are not against us are with us." The party began to accept that it would have to make do with formal compliance. It would have to abandon its previous totalitarian--in the literal sense--demands for allegiance, control and commitment in all spheres, public and even private.[1] This tacit acceptance of withdrawal of the party from some spheres was in itself a new element that pointed towards a new strategy by those who opposed the party's control. A form of power sharing became thinkable once the party abandoned its totalitarian claims on society.

These developments were lent support by the opening up of central European countries in this period. Legitimisation would now depend on providing sufficient economic success,[2] which required access to western capital, technology and consumer goods. Another key political safety valve was to allow citizens freedom to travel to the west. This went farthest soonest in Hungary. Conversely, western tourism in central Europe was a valuable source of scarce hard currency. Those contacts permitted comparison and a more open attitude in society, which challenged the party and encouraged the creation of independent space not controlled by the party.

A fundamental external development, ironically strongly encouraged by Moscow, was the signature of the CSCE Helsinki Final Act in 1975.[3] The USSR had wanted a pan-European Agreement that would endorse the Yalta status quo in central Europe. The west accepted this in principle, with the proviso that *peaceful* change in the status quo should not be ruled out. At the same time, the western states in the CSCE process insisted on adding the so-called "third basket" to the agreement. This "third basket" was initially modest in scope, referring only to limited issues such as family reunification and increasing human contacts, but gradually expanded by virtue of its linkage with two of the basic principles of the Helsinki Final Act:[4] "Respect for human rights and fundamental freedoms, including freedom of thought, conscience, religion or conviction" and "equality of peoples and their right of self-determination." By the Vienna Follow-Up Conference Document (1986), this general language had been tightened up to include an obligation to "guarantee to everyone the right to know his rights and obligations and to act on them and to that end to publish and make accessible legislation and procedures relating to human rights and fundamental freedoms" (paragraph 13(4)) and to "respect the right of their citizens to contribute actively individually or in association with others to the promotion and protection of human rights and fundamental freedoms" (paragraph 13(5)).

Initially, the Soviet Union and its Central European allies regarded these commitments as a purely symbolic and unimportant price to pay for their main aims in the geopolitical sphere. Furthermore, they sought to argue that the principles on human rights, read as the Final Act required with the other principles, including non-intervention in internal affairs, remained an internal matter. The term "non-intervention," insisted on by the western states, came to be understood as less restrictive than the usual diplomatic term "non-interference."[5]

As a result, human rights in central Europe became an international matter of concern to the whole CSCE community, which could become part of the on-going follow-up processes of the CSCE. Internally, it became permissible to seek compliance with the Helsinki obligations without moving into overt subversion or anti-regime activity. Such requests were, after all, in theory, "sanctioned" by the central European states themselves by their act of signing the Helsinki documents. At the same time, collective action to promote respect for the Helsinki principles and contact with similar groups in other signatory states should also have been permitted and not considered subversive. This was a major change and opened the door to the activities of Helsinki monitoring groups acting both clandestinely and semi-legally, often with the support of governments and activists in the west. This kind of narrow issue-oriented, semi-legal approach fit exactly with the new doctrines of developing elements of civil society as autonomous space not controlled by the party. It did so by referring to principles which furthermore transcended the party and which offered alternatives to the official ideology, without entering into a direct confrontation with its pretension to rule.[6]

The Helsinki process also opened up "space" in another crucial dimension that was later to be exploited amply in the Gorbachev era. As one observer argued, the Helsinki process "created a framework for articulating and accommodating conflicting interests *not only* [author's emphasis] between east

and west but also between the Europeans and their respective super-power."
It also allowed "informal alignments cutting across established political
patterns and ideological barriers."[7] This was a crucial development towards
a revival of a central European consciousness and stirrings of greater
autonomy.

Poland led the way in this phase, both in developing the new thinking and
in practising it.[8] In 1968, workers in Poland had offered no support for
intellectuals. In the 1970 riots in Gdansk, intellectuals held aloof. The key
new development in 1976 was the alliance between the industrial workers
primarily on the Baltic coast and the intellectuals who formed the KOR or
Workers Defence Committee (later the Social Defence Committee) to support
those arrested and victimized after the events--including strikes against the
1976 price rises, which the government was to withdraw. Out of this alliance
came the idea of an independent trade union as a social movement that sought
to establish independent space rather than challenge the party directly. The
support of the powerful Catholic church, headed dramatically from 1978 by
a Polish Pope, was also a key factor, establishing in 1980-1981 a new
equilibrium in Polish society between three factors--Solidarity (Solidarnosc),
the Church and the party. For almost eighteen months, a body with 10
million members existed outside the control of the party. This was a seminal
development.

Though it appeared to fail in the short-term, this experience could not help
but send major reverberations throughout the whole of Central Europe,
showing as it did the new approach in action. It reinforced the emergent
social and human rights movement, which was taking the Helsinki Final Act
as its reference and starting point, and moving into the ideological void
created by the withdrawal of the communist parties into "negative
legitimation"[9] and forms of technocratic management. Part of the new
equation, especially in Hungary, but also in Slovakia, was the shift to
legitimation by economic success--at least of a relative kind. Clearly, were
the economic pillar of the regime to weaken, then a new strategy would have
to be developed by the parties in power.

A new anti-politics emerged, based on moral considerations, emphasizing
human dignity, human rights, truth and the creation of autonomous space not
under the hegemony of the party. This "space" was at one and the same time
conceived of as a moral end in itself and also a means whereby (as, briefly,
in Poland in 1980-1981,) the party might be obliged to enter into a dialogue
with society. The exponents of those ideas were writers and intellectuals. In
Poland, there were Lesak Kolakowski,[10] Jacek Kuron,[11] Adam Michnik;[12] in

Hungary, György Konrad,[13] and Janos Kis;[14] and in Czechoslovakia, above all, Vaclav Havel[15] and Jan Patočka,[16] the first leader of Charter 77, who died under police interrogation. These currents gave rise to Charter 77 and the Hungarian dissident movement that both later linked up with environmentalists in the Danube circle in opposition to the Gabčikovo-Nagymaros project. By the mid-1980s, with the emergence of perestroika, those tendencies found themselves (at least in Hungary though not in conservative Czechoslovakia) in a paradoxical dialectic with party reformers, who were trying to save the system by forcing it to evolve.

We shall now turn to look at the developments, first in Hungary, then in Czechoslovakia, in more detail. Though, in each it is important not to lose sight of the wider regional and geopolitical environment. External factors were vital, especially insofar as that they eventually swept away the cautious party reformers as irrelevant.

Hungary was, after 1958 and as we have seen, characterised by a continuous economic reformism and negative legitimation that made up Kadarism. Despite the active support of the Hungarian minority in Slovakia for the Prague Spring, the events of 1968 passed Hungary by.[17] By the early 1980s, the Hungarian model was coming to the end of its capacity for development. Kadar, like Gomulka, was unable to evolve. The system had become fossilized.

The same was true in the economic field. With the need to open the economy to the west came, inevitably, the opening of the hitherto closed economy, at least partially, to the cyclical vagaries of the world economy in the wake of the oil crisis. This brought inflation, debt and recession to the Hungarian economy and undermined the economic legitimisation that the regime had gained since the economic reforms. Economic reform without more radical structural change and hence without political change had run its course and was unable to respond to the new challenges of an economy partially vulnerable to the recession of the world economy.[18] Gorbachev's ascent to power, his doctrine of glasnost and perestroika and his cautious abandonment of the Brezhnev doctrine appeared to offer at least a potential way out of the impasse, which some Hungarian Party reformers had been quietly considering even before Gorbachev:[19] a new reformist policy that would re-legitimise the leadership and redynamise the economy without leading to the collapse of the regime. This would lead to some form of genuine and permanent power-sharing with society, greater pluralism and withdrawal of the party from its totalitarian pretensions in many areas of society.[20] This would have corresponded with the new thinking of oppositionists such as Konrad and Kis. It was in Hungary that this eminently Gorbachevian approach came closest to working, because there it began early and had some not inconsiderable indigenous roots and hence greater credibility. Indeed, had Hungary been able to evolve in a vacuum, it might have succeeded in installing a semi-democratic system, where the party retained most of the levers of political power. It was paradoxically the "bridge too far" in the Gorbachevian thinking--namely, abandonment of the Brezhnev doctrine *before* reformists had become installed--that effectively torpedoed this reformist strategy. Indeed, without the Brezhnev doctrine and Soviet threat, the self-denying ordinance in place since 1956 was no longer needed.

The "Wende" in Hungary was long and gradual and began well before even the second legalisation of Solidarnosc in Poland. By about 1985, the regime had begun to lose the support, not only of old "dissidents" but also of previously loyal intellectuals and technocrats. In 1986, for example, a group of "insider" economists published a critique entitled "Turning Point and Reform," calling for more radical economic reforms.[21] Attempts were made to establish independent trade unions. Once Kadar had been removed in May 1988, the long latent divisions in the party leadership emerged and created a near paralysis as debate raged between those who believed that "Kadarism without Kadar" was a viable option and those who recognised, however tentatively, that the new departures were needed if the Communist Party was to retain any role at all.[22] Hungary had, since the end of the post-1956 repression, a regime that was in many ways already "soft," and much was tolerated without being approved.[23]

Thus, as early as 1983-1984, mainly for environmental reasons, groups began to form to oppose the Nagymaros Dam, which were, in 1984, to become known as the Danube Circle, in which the environmentalist journalist Janos Vargha played such a key role. This Danube movement was able to collect 10,000 signatures and hold meetings, rallies and demonstrations. It forced the government to re-examine the project and to allow the open vote in Parliament in 1988 that, though, confirmed the project. Then, finally, it organised a massive 140,000 signature petition as the dam became the symbol of the regime itself. Ultimately, the Nemeth (still communist) government suspended work on the project in May 1989.[24] A very large number of Hungarians gradually became involved in opposition activities. During this period, other opposition groups were also forming, in particular SZETA (Foundation for the Poor). These other groups cooperated with Duna Kör in opposing the Dam, which became a symbolic rallying point for all opposition. One evaluation puts the combined Hungarian opposition as second only to the Polish in its extent during this period.[25]

The first sign that change was in the air came with the 1985 election at which 704 party candidates (more than the seats to be filled) and for the first time, 77 independent candidates, stood. Twenty five independents were elected.[26] The thirtieth anniversary of 1956 saw an open debate for the first time. It was a key sign. Karoly Grooss, a moderate, replaced Kadarist Premier Lazar in June 1987. A head of stream was building up for more radical change. In June 1987, the Samizdat Journal published a new political programme of the opposition, drafted by Janos Kis, entitled "Social Contract." It called for the dismissal of Kadar and a compromise between the party that would retain its authority over foreign policy and defence.[27] Parliament would be restored, but the party would retain a veto power. This was very similar to the Polish 1989 Round Table compromise that led to the first semi-democratic elections in central Europe.

The next key move came from within the party apparatus. Mihaly Bihar, then advisor to Imre Poszgay, leading reformer and in 1987 Chairman of the Patriotic Front, drew up a report entitled "Reform and Democracy." This report proposed a radical political reform as the only way out of the current stalemate. He called for the separation of the party and state, restoration of the role of law, as in the old Habsburg Empire, reinvigoration of the Parliament and establishment of a constitutional court. Without saying so, Bihar was promoting pluralism and ending the leading role of the party.[28] In fact, Poszgay was an early exponent of Gorbachevism and even took it further by preempting moderate opposition demands, so making the political running in advance of the opposition.[29]

At the same time, a law was passed permitting the establishment of independent groups, provided that they were not officially political parties. By the autumn of 1987, even this restriction disappeared in practice and a number of new political movements began to appear. The MDF (Hungarian Democratic Forum), led by Jozsef Antall, was formed in September 1987, bringing together nationalists, populists, Christian Democrats and occupying a "centrist" position between the ruling Communist Party and the more radical opposition groupings. By 1989, the MDF had become more of a Volkspartei on the German/Austrian model and had broken with the reform communists. The Alliance of Free Democrats (SDS) was formed by intellectuals and human rights activists at the same period as a more radical opposition. The Federation of Young Democrats (FIDESZ) was set up in March 1988 under the leadership of Viktor Orban, originally as a youth organisation. It was intended to be "new" and young.[30]

All this happened while Kadar was still in power, but now the stage was set for his removal at the Party Congress held on May 20-22, 1988. The Prime Minister, Karoly Grosz, was elected First Secretary and in November, he stepped down as Prime Minister, to be replaced by a far more committed reformer, the young Harvard-educated economist, Miklos Nemeth. The power struggle and with it the battle for the political course for Hungary was very far from over. Indeed, it had just begun.[31]

A new phenomenon now re-entered the stage and was a useful consensus-building device at this crucial phase--nationalism. During the Kadar era, the regime had been persistently reluctant to let out the genie of nationalism, directed against other People's Democracies where Hungarians lived, such as Yugoslavia, Czechoslovakia and above all, Romania. Hungarians had never emotionally accepted the Trianon boundaries that were reimposed after 1945. In the 1980s, nationalism also began to re-emerge in the neighbouring states as a tool of regime legitimisation. This involved measures that were or seemed threatening to the local Hungarian minorities along the Danube in Slovakia, in the Banat, in Transylvania or the Voivodina. The situation became the most dramatic in Romania, with the Ceaucescu regime adopting an early form of "ethnic cleansing" against its German and Hungarian minorities. The Siebenburgen Germans had a rich and powerful protector in the Federal Republic. Could Hungary ignore the repression of Hungarians and the arrival of refugees from over the Romanian border? Strikes took place in the mining areas of Transylvania in 1977, 1983 and 1987 and were savagely suppressed. On November 15, 1987, a demonstration of 20,000 workers took place in Brasov, centre of the German-speaking minority, against restrictions on heating and electricity. There were similar demonstrations in Hungarian centres such as Cluj, Temesvar, Arad and Jassy. From 1983, the Hungarian press had begun to report such issues. Between 1987 and 1988, over 25,000 Hungarian refugees came across the border. The Hungarians raised the issue at the CSCE in April 1988 and in June 1988, a silent demonstration of 100,000 people was authorised in Budapest. Several rounds of negotiations between the two communist leaderships failed to achieve any progress. Nationalism was back.[32]

Alongside the prudent, measured official reform, a spontaneous, chaotic reform process took off as old organisations and parties were revived. Otto von Habsburg was received in the Hungarian Parliament. His mother, the last Empress Zita, was given a funeral ceremony in the cathedral in April 1989.

In June, Imre Nagy was rehabilitated in a vast ceremony. On June 24th, a new collective leadership of the party was installed with four members chaired by Nyers, with Poszgay, Nemeth and the new relatively Conservative Secretary-General Grosz. A congress was called on October 6. Victories by MDF candidates in four parliamentary by-elections in July kept up the pressure. There were also dramatic events in foreign policy after the reformist Gyula Horn took over as Foreign Minister in April 1989. He dismantled the Iron Curtain border with neutral Austria along its 350 km length in May. In the summer and early autumn, he allowed GDR citizens, ostensibly "tourists," to escape into Austria, hastening the fall of the Berlin Wall. In November, the Hungarian government applied for membership of the Council of Europe. By now, Poland had overtaken Hungary by holding semi-democratic elections and forming a Solidarnosc government.[33]

The Party Congress of October 6 brought the final dénouement in the power struggle. Those who believed in pre-emptive action now won their chance, though in the event it was too late, as it might not have been one year earlier. The Hungarian Socialist Workers' Party (communist) was dissolved and became the Hungarian Socialist Party (MSZP). Fewer than 200 of the 1,259 delegates opposed this move. Rezsö Nyers was elected leader. The MSZP was still divided between the centrists of Nyers, the reformists of Poszgay and the communists of Grosz and Berecz. Soon, the Grosz current split and with traditionalists held a "real" 14th Congress and reconstituted the HSWP in December 1989.[34]

The way was open for free elections, but even now, the process was slow and deliberate. Parliament began the process of reforming the Constitution. Hungary became a Republic (no longer a People's Republic). A Presidency of the Republic was created. The main issue was how the President should be elected: by the people, as the MSZP wanted, or by Parliament after the first free elections in 1990, as the opposition wanted? The reform communists wanted this apparently more democratic solution so as to capitalise on their better known leaders. The opposition blocked this move by organising a massive petition (206,000 signatures) and forcing a referendum. 50.1 percent voted against the popular election option and 45 percent abstained.[35] A Round Table between the old leadership and the new opposition parties agreed on the main political parameters: a limited Presidency elected by Parliament; two-thirds majority requirements for constitutional and organic legislation; a two-ballot electoral system in 176 single-member constituencies with a regional (152) and national (58) top-up seats from lists. There were some severe anti-splitting rules. Nominees in single-member seats required 750 signatures of voters. A national list could only be presented if the party stood in at least seven of the twenty regions (with 4-28 seats) and there was a 4 percent threshold for the distribution of regional and national list seats.[36] These arrangements were put in place as early as September 1989.

The transition was so long and gradual when compared to other states in the region, such as Czechoslovakia, the GDR and Romania, that the elections seemed an anti-climax when they finally did come in March and April 1990.[37] Clearly, people supported the changes, but without much mobilisation. Turnout was only 65 percent in the first round and less (45 percent) in the second.

The MDF, a popular "volkspartei" of the centre right, became a catch-all party,[38] appealing to all social groups and all regions. It was ahead in the constituency contests in 80 seats and in the second round won in 114, gaining votes from all of the eliminated smaller parties in run-offs (where the top *three* could stand), either with the Alliance of Free Democrats or the Young Democrats. The Free Democrats gained their voters among young and middle-aged, well-educated urban groups, especially in Budapest and in the northwest, such as Györ. The other "Liberal Party," the FIDESZ (8.9 percent), performed as the polls predicted. Its votes came from the same groups as the SDS, but were from a younger stratum. The Christian Democrats (6.5 percent) did well. Their vote was mainly in villages or provincial towns from elderly, less educated Catholic women. It did best in the Catholic northwest and northeast. The historical Smallholders' Party[39] achieved only a poor result in line with the general failure in Hungary, and indeed all over central Europe, of revived parties. It won only 4.7 percent (even below its poll forecasts). It gained no votes in the second round, remaining stuck in the rut of its narrow sectional electorate. It won its votes in the historic strongholds of the party in mid-south Hungary. It won its best support among less educated men living in rural areas. The MSZP, with 10.9 percent, did much as expected, but it failed to win any constituency seats; hence, it was under-represented in Parliament. Its main support was in Budapest, industrial regions and in Protestant areas. The old HSWP won only negligible levels of support. The revived Social Democrats, with 3.5 percent, failed to win any seats. A scattering of agrarians (2) and independents also won a small number of seats (10 in all).

The MDF had shown itself the best adapted to the complex electoral system, especially in terms of mobilising additional support between the two ballots. Thus, in MDF/SDS duels (125 seats), the MDF increased its vote by 29.1 percent and the SDS by only 5 percent. Thus, the SDS only won 35 seats of the 63 in which it was ahead after the first ballot, of which 23 were in Budapest. A tri-polar bloc structure emerged with the centre-right MDF, Smallholders and Christian Democrats; Liberal-left SDS-FIDESZ and Socialist-left MSZP/HSWP:[40]

	Seats	*Percent*
MDF	164	(42.49)
SDS	92	(23.80)
Smallholders (SHP)	44	(11.40)
MSZP	33	(8.60)
FIDESZ	22	(5.70)
Christian Democrats (CDP)	21	(5.40)
HSWP	0	3.65
SDP	0	3.55
Others	10	2.50

This enabled the centre right MDF/SHP/CDP coalition, with 229 seats (total 386) under the MDF leader, Jozsef Antall, to be formed. Though this coalition (208 seats) would have mustered an adequate majority, a deal was made with the opposition SDS to elect its leader President and to enact jointly certain constitutional measures for which a two-thirds majority was required. This centre-right coalition actually offered a more gradual, more "Hungarian" transition, based on traditional national populist values, as against the "cosmopolitanism" of the SDS and FIDESZ. It was the old Hungarian Kulturkampf.

Hungarian parties were fragile and highly personalised. The Smallholders' Party soon became embroiled in a byzantine internal power struggle and split in several directions;[41] elections and by-elections saw gains for the SDS in the larger cities and the MSZP in the countryside, as popular alienation from politics grew more serious. The very breadth of the MDF, an advantage in winning the election in 1990, became a serious problem. Tensions developed from 1992, between the centrist leadership of the MDF and the rightist/populist wing of the party that crystallised around the party's Vice-Chairman, Istvan Csurka. He wrote an infamous article on August 20, 1992 in the Magyar Forum, of which he was the editor, openly expressing views that he and other populist such as the writer Csoori had been preparing from some time. He attacked what he called the "secret clauses" of agreements with the AFD opposition and with the IMF that bound, he said, the Antall government. He put forward a conspiracy theory involving the

IMF, liberals, Jews and the old communists. He proposed a populist Hungarian, anti-western middle way. Csurka formed the Magyar Ut (Hungarian Way) Movement to promote his populist ideas and entered into a power struggle with Prime Minister Antall. At the MDF Congress of January 23, 1993, his line was defeated, though his supporters won 5 of 21 Presidium seats. At that time, he announced that he would leave the MDF after the elections. The leadership struck back and expelled Csurka and his supporters in June 1993 and at the same time, expelled the liberal faction around Dbréczeni, who wanted closer cooperation with the SDS. In November 1993, Csurka founded a new party, the Hungarian Truth (MIEP), which eleven MDF MPs joined, but which actually won a derisory 1.58 percent in the 1994 elections.[42] Some kind of alternative centre-left coalition became almost inevitable following the death of Prime Minister Antall, the main cement of the MDF.

Czechoslovakia remained quiescent during the whole period of progress towards reform in both Poland and Hungary. A very conservative Slovak-dominated leadership remained in place from the post-Prague Spring normalisation right up to the "events" of November 1989. The change from Husak to Jakeš in late 1987, with Husak retaining the Presidency of the Republic, was of no real significance. The gradual loss of intellectual support was much more telescoped in Czechoslovakia. Unlike Poland and Hungary, dissidence was a very narrow intellectual, even Prague-based, phenomenon. It did not mobilise workers, nor did it achieve any mass support. Furthermore, it was almost exclusively a Czech phenomenon. Slovakia was relatively well treated during the "normalisation" years.[43] It retained its "acquis" from the Prague Spring, federalisation. The party purge was less severe. Slovak leaders obtained significant positions in Prague for the first time and significant investments were channelled into Slovakia. The Gabčikovo-Nagymaros dam project--a vital Slovak concern--was undertaken.

Yet, in a deeper sense, the disillusion provoked by the failure of the Prague Spring, though on the surface it seemed to produce only passivity and alienation, was important. After 1968, any new generation of oppositionists could not adopt Marxism or Socialism, even with a "human face," as their reference point.[44] Nor could the party be considered as an instrument for reform. These considerations determined the special characteristics of Czech oppositional thinking and organisation. Unlike in Hungary and Poland, there was no reform party within the party. Indeed, on the contrary, for the hard-line Party leadership, the 1968 experience became a constant point of reference *against* reform.[45] Yet, by 1987, there was some evidence that the

Soviet leadership was becoming concerned about the rigidity of the Czechoslovak Party. Some now see the decision to support or accept Jakeš, rather than another more likely reformer such as Lubomir Strougal, to follow Husak as Party Leader as a serious mistake.[46]

The regime was not, as yet, under serious internal challenge, but clearly it was incapable of regaining support. Havel's concept of "living in truth," his exultation over the potential "power of the powerless" and the coming together in Charter 77 of those who felt along the same lines in early 1977 was not the basis of a mass movement but undoubtedly it was saying articulately what a large part of the population knew instinctively, even if they were not willing or able to join the dissident movement. This "Svejkist" behaviour was dangerous, in that it could and did lull an unwary and fossilised leadership into the comfortable belief that the regime did have adequate resources to survive an external shock.

Thus, down to the beginning of 1989, Czechoslovakia seemed stable and unlikely to see any major upset. From the beginning of 1989,[47] the pressure increased. There was the changing international environment and the emulation effect of what was happening in Hungary, Poland and even the USSR. From June onwards, there was the dramatic impact of the exodus of East Germans, some of whom took temporary refuge in the West German Embassy in Prague. At the same time, the dissidents were at last reaching a wider audience and mobilising a larger section of public opinion, in particular the students.

In January 1989, there was a five-day wave of demonstrations to commemorate the self-immolation of Jan Palach twenty years earlier. Vaclav Havel was arrested and convicted and then released under international pressure. A human rights petition was gathered and presented in June with 1,800 signatures. Cardinal Tomasek offered in August to mediate between the opposition and the state. Despite impressive security and pre-emptive arrests, several thousand people demonstrated on Wenceslas Square on August 21, anniversary of the Soviet invasion. Independence Day on October 28 saw Havel detained again and a demonstration of 10,000 people. After November 9 and the fall of the Wall in Berlin, the Czech government also reduced restrictions on travel to the west. Calls from the opposition for mass demonstrations redoubled in Prague, Brno and Bratislava.

There is still some mystery surrounding the demonstration of 30,000 people in Prague on November 17, 1989, that became the "coup d'envoi" for the so-called velvet revolution. This demonstration, unlike others, was actually authorised. It was to commemorate the death of a student, Jan

Opletal, at the hands of the Nazis in 1939. The official demonstration was as it were hijacked and became an anti-regime demonstration. A student was reported killed and there were severe beatings and arrests. One theory is that the "student" was an agent of the security police and that the whole repression and even hijacking of the demonstration was a "mise en scène" by elements in the security forces, in cooperation with the Soviet KGB, with the aim of destabilising the conservative leadership and replacing it by a Gorbachevian team in Czechoslovakia.[48] If this were so, it was by now in any case too late.

The velvet revolution was continued over the coming days by mass demonstrations, strikes, rallies and meetings, which gradually came to be orchestrated by the students at Charles University. Leadership was then more importantly taken over by a broad umbrella opposition organisation led by Vaclav Havel, with which Dubček was also associated; the Civic Forum (OF) and its Slovak counterpart, the Public Against Violence (VNP). OF and VNP became interlocuteurs of the party.[49] The replacement of Jakeš, the resignation of the whole Politburo, modest proposals for a more reformist government all failed to regain the initiative for the party. Thus, by December 10, OF and VPN and the mass movement behind them forced the resignation of the Adamec Cabinet and its replacement by the Slovak reformist Marian Čalfa at the head of a "national unity" cabinet, including former dissidents such as Jan Komarek at the Economics Ministry and Jiri Dienstbier as Foreign Minister. The new government dissolved the security police and dismantled the Iron Curtain to Austria. The "leading role" of the Communist Party was removed from the Constitution. Using obscure recall procedures, Dubček became a Deputy to the National Assembly and then speaker and so presided over the election of Vaclav Havel as President of the Republic on December 29, 1989.

Elections were set for June 8-9, 1990. The round table between the OF, VNP and other political parties established an expert commission to make proposals on the electoral system. Several variants were studied, but in the end, it was decided to use the party list system that was used in the first Republic and in 1946.[50] Radical measures, such as a constituency system, (later supported by elements within OF), reduction of the number of deputies or abolition of the Upper House, were not pursued as they were too controversial. There was though some departure from a "pure" list system. Parties needed to show support from 10,000 voters in order to stand. There was a 5 percent electoral threshold, reduced to 3 percent for the Slovak National Council only. Seats were allocated within 12 regional constituencies and remaining seats were then allocated within each Republic by the highest remainder system. Citizens voted simultaneously but separately for the Federal

National Assembly (150 seats), for the 75 seats in the Upper House from "their" Republic and third for the Czech or Slovak National Council, depending on where they resided.[51]

There was a blossoming of new and resuscitated political parties. Sixty six met legal registration requirements. Twenty two tabled lists but only 11 tabled nationwide lists. Three old parties, including the Communist Party, stood. Many, including the Electoral Grouping for Interest Associations (bee keepers, animal breeders, anglers, gardeners), Friends of Beer Party, Movement for Civic Freedom (gay activists, etc.) seemed unlikely to meet the 5 percent threshold. There were distinctive Slovak parties, Greens, minority parties and the Regionalist Society for Moravia and Silesia. Few doubted that OF and VPN would succeed, but these newer parties remained an unknown quantity. Many commentators noted the bland and general sameness of the party programmes. All stood for social security, the market economy, equal status for private ownership, ecology, return to Europe. All parties were given four hours (!) of TV time and there were two TV roundtable debates. These did little to differentiate the parties. OF and VPN were a very broad church. The Christian Democrats were centrists. In essence, the election was a referendum on Communism, with the result a foregone conclusion.[52] As Havel himself said, it was a "dress rehearsal" for the next election in two year's time, which would see the party system crystallise.[53]

Turnout was a massive 96 percent, with fairly clear victories, as expected, for OF and VPN, though VPN did much less well in Slovakia (32.34 percent for the Federal Assembly's House of the People) than OF (53.15 percent) in the Czech Republic. Less expected was the quite good result of the communists and the Moravian/Silesian list (8.79 percent). OF and VPN did win a majority of seats in both Houses, but not the "constituent" three-fifths majority. This was later to prove a serious problem. Nor did VPN win an overall majority in the Slovak National Council. Results in the Czech Republic's National Council and for the Czech seats in the House of Nations were very similar. This was less so in Slovakia. The VPN won a considerably lower share, with 29.3 percent for the Slovak National Council. With a 3 percent threshold, more parties qualified. The Slovak National Party won 2 percent more than for the Federal Parliament. A coalition of VPN and the Slovak Christian Democrat Movement was the only possibility in Slovakia. Results were:[54]

I. House of the People (150 seats)

a) Czech Republic (101 seats)	*% vote*	*Seats*
OF	53.15	68
Communists	13.48	15
Christian & Democratic Union	8.69	9
Society for Moravia & Silesia	7.89	9
Others	16.79	0

b) Slovak Republic (49 seats)		
VPN	32.54	19
Christian Democratic Movement	18.96	11
Communists	13.81	8
Slovak National Party	10.95	6
Co-existence	8.58	5
Others	15.15	0

II. House of Nations (150 seats)

a) Czech Republic (75 seats)	*% vote*	*Seats*
OF	49.96	50
Communists	13.80	12
Christian & Democratic Union	8.75	6
Society for Moravia & Silesia	9.10	7
Others	18.39	0

b) Slovak Republic (75 seats)		
VPN	37.28	33
Christian Democratic Movement	16.66	14
Communists	13.43	12
Slovak National Party	11.44	9
Co-existence	8.49	7
Others	12.70	

Similar coalitions of OF and the Christian Democrats or VPN and Christian Democrats were formed in all three governments--Federal, Czech and Slovak--giving a broad political and national base and the necessary "constituent" majority in both Houses of the Federal Parliament and in both Republic delegations in the House of Nations.

Such broad umbrella parties with weak organisation and no clear positive ideology other than generalised support for democracy and the market economy could not hold together under the strains of practical governing. Their leaders soon diverged over key questions such as the pace of market reform and constitutional issues such as Czech/Slovak relations or the powers of the President. This led to tensions and splits. This was hardly surprising, given the speed with which OF had grown, its lack of structure and its broad base, including radical market liberals, social democrats, reform communists and Trotskyists. Within OF, there was too a diametrically opposed view about its future. Some considered that it had played its role and should evolve into a normal political party, if necessary splitting in the process. Others remained committed to the idea of a broad moral "anti-party" movement.[55] At the same time, the rise of Slovak nationalism as a political force was pulling VPN away from OF.

The first democratic government ran for almost two years until the elections held in May 1992. It failed to resolve the issues of constitutional reform: reform of the federation, the powers of the Presidency, the electoral system. President Havel's proposals for a stronger presidency close to the French model were rejected. Havel argued for continued federation. He therefore became a figure of suspicion in Slovakia. His sincere opposition to separatist tendencies was seen as anti-Slovak, a continuation of First Republic and even communist attitudes towards Slovakia. In Prague, the more radical market reformers became concerned at the moderation and gradualism of Havel and those close to him in the old OF. They founded a more radical market reform party (Civic Party ODS) under Finance Minister Vaclav Klaus.[56]

The second election confirmed these centrifugal tendencies, with different outcomes in the Czech and Slovak Republics, following a quite different process of political realignment that preceded the election. In the Czech Republic, the Civil Democratic Party (ODS) of Klaus was the victor in the June 1992 elections. He easily defeated the other ex-components of the OF and in particular the Civil Democrats Movement (ODH) led by Jiri Dienstbier, and close to President Havel. In Slovakia, the VPN had split. Its leader, Vladimir Mečiar, had been over thrown as Prime Minister and formed his own party, the Democratic Slovakia Movement (HZDS), which had been joined by some Christian Democrats. The HZDS won 74 of the 150 seats in the Slovak National Council and emerged as the largest party. This movement was increasingly nationalist and favoured a much slower transition to a market economy. The Czech and Slovak republics were moving in opposite directions.[57] Those who favoured union, the old VPN, Christian Democrats, the ODH and President Havel, emerged weakened from the elections and a compromise came to look like squaring the circle. The Slovak deputies now refused to re-elect Vaclav Havel. On July 17, 1992, 113 deputies voted for Slovak sovereignty. On July 23 and 24, Mečiar and Klaus met in Bratislava to consider the future of the state and agreed on dissolution and hence independence for Slovakia as from January 1, 1993.

Let us look back at how that irrevocable and by then seemingly inevitable outcome had been reached.[58] The prolonged and rancorous debate about the name of the state--hyphenated or not--was a bad sign. It raised the question of how far the Czech side was indeed ready to make a new start in Czech/Slovak relations, rectifying its past errors. It soon became clear that little had changed. As one Slovak deputy, Mr. Anton Hrnko put it, "the Czech side, just like Masaryk and his successors, refused to discuss anything except what they themselves proposed."[59] Four main meetings were held between August 1990 and June 1991. One of these was prepared by no less than three other meetings, involving Havel personally. At the Kromeriz meeting on June 17, 1991, it was agreed that a commission should prepare a text of a treaty between the two republics, which would be the basis of future relations. This text would be adopted by both National Councils and the Federal parliament before the end of 1991. The review meeting held on November 12 made no progress. The Czechs presented no text, whilst the Slovaks published their own proposals on December 28, 1991. Havel failed on January 21, 1992, to gain parliamentary approval for his proposal for a referendum. The text belatedly agreed by representatives of the two National Councils at Milovy on February 4 was rejected by the Slovak National Council on February 25. It was a dialogue of the deaf. Now, no further progress could be made before the elections. The atmosphere became more tense and in the election campaign the debate was polarised in the two Republics.

In the Slovak language, there are two terms for "sovereignty": "Zvrchovanost," which means the right to self-determination, but does not necessarily mean independent statehood; and "Suvrenita," which means independence under international law.[60] For many in the Slovak debate, the question was how to obtain the first without necessarily proceeding to the second. Thus, the Slovak proposals of December 28, 1991, proposed four options: (a) the present federal system, (b) a common state based on a treaty, with a Slovak President, a confederation based on a Treaty or (d) a confederation with other European states. Given the increasing internal pressure, with demonstrations in support of sovereignty organised by the Matica Slovenska and the political configuration in the Slovak National council even before the 1992 elections, only some form of confederation was acceptable to Slovakia, though few except the Slovak National Party (SNS) would have then actively preferred full independence. The election strongly reinforced this trend.

On the Czech side, the Left (former communists and the Social Democrats, represented in Parliament after the 1992 elections) and the Havel faction opposed weakening the federation, though they sought to reach at least some compromise with the Slovaks. They proposed a referendum to demonstrate that public opinion opposed the break-up of the Czechoslovak State in both Republics, and by that sought to block that option as a "default option," so obliging radicals on both sides to compromise. Klaus and his supporters were not prepared to make concessions that would water down their market reforms and provide subsidies from the strong Czech economy to the weaker Slovakia or that would slow down the return to Europe.[61] For Klaus, a confederation with complex blocking mechanisms and economic transfers would represent the worst of all possible worlds. Given the two options that were reinforced by the election--a reformed but still centralised and market-oriented federation or independence on the Czech side and at a minimum confederation and independence on the Slovak side, separation became the only consensual option. Even so, it was probably rejected by majorities of the voters in both Republics and had not been the first choice of most political leaders. Klaus himself may soon have come to see the departure of Slovakia as a good outcome and the alternatives as worse and hence have called the Slovaks' bluff, obliging them to seek independence.[62] Thus, on January 1, 1993, Slovakia became a new independent nation, with a parliamentary system. A Protestant, Mr. Kovacs, was elected President and Mr. Mečiar continued as Prime Minister. All parties, except the Hungarian minority parties, voted for the constitution. At first, the HZDS governed in a coalition with the SNS, but the Economics Minister from the SNS resigned over the pace of reform, which he wanted to accelerate. The opposition was split between left and right, making it relatively easy for the HZDS minority cabinet to survive, despite several more defections. Eventually, in November 1993, a new HZDS/SNS coalition was formed, but even that did not bring much greater political stability. However, that government sought to create a broad majority for the nation-building process. The Czech "enemy" is gone with independence, but the Hungarian "enemy" remains and this is an important factor in the dispute over Gabčikovo-Nagymaros. Indeed, the Slovaks are well aware that the Hungarians had hoped that the post-1989 Czechoslovak government would impose a stop to the project. Gabčikovo is a potent symbol of the Slovak nation and its continuation is thus seen as a victory over both Prague and Budapest. The position of the Hungarian minority in that context remains very difficult. Few Slovaks are sympathetic to the minority. Some point out that Hungarians offer no reciprocal rights to Slovaks in Hungary or to Slovaks who are minorities in Hungarian communities in Slovakia.[63]

The issue of the Hungarian minority remains a difficult one, and is closely linked to the Gabčikovo-Nagymaros issue, as the Hungarian minority lives in the Danube basin and is significantly affected by the dam. The position of the minority is also a serious apple of discord in Slovak-Hungarian relations. Indeed, Hungary initially attempted to block Slovakia's membership of the Council of Europe on that ground. The minority was in a difficult situation in the First Republic, worsened in the 1945-1948 period, improved modestly between 1948-1968 and then significantly during the Prague Spring and again briefly in 1989-1990. Now, according to Co-existence, the main party of the minority, it has deteriorated again in the face of Slovak nation-building: "The political changes following November 1989 resulted in significant improvements in the general human rights and freedoms provided by Slovakia. As far as the legal rights of national minorities are concerned, however, the situation has worsened" (at least until the new Moravčik coalition took power.)[64]

Already, in the First Republic of 1920-1938, the Hungarians--then 1 million (21.7 percent)--considered themselves victims of severe discrimination, though they could organise politically and culturally. Over 105,000 left voluntarily or were forced into exile in 1920. It is claimed that language legislation and the higher education system in particular were discriminatory. After the return of the areas inhabited by the minority to Czechoslovakia in 1945, a number of severely repressive measures were introduced, though the Potsdam Conference did not authorise the deportation of 200,000 Hungarians, as requested by the Czechoslovaks. Measures were taken to limit minority rights and property. Citizenship was lost unless minority members renounced their minority status and accepted "re-slovakisation." Some 70,000 were deported or resettled elsewhere. Under an Exchange of Population Agreement signed on February 17, 1946, another 75,000 Hungarian minority members left Slovakia.[65]

During the communist period, the pressure on the minority eased, in order to avoid conflict between two People's Democracies, but assimilation continued. By the 1950 census, the minority represented 10.5 percent of the population, recovered to 12.4 percent in 1961 but declined to 10.8 percent in 1991. The communist constitution of 1960 guaranteed "every possibility and means for native language education and cultural development of citizens of Hungarian, Ukrainian and Polish nationality." During the Prague Spring, a more far-reaching law was adopted, which guaranteed cultural development, the use of their language in administration, press and media for the minority languages and most significantly, recognised the Hungarians as a "state-forming" nation. In the context of post-1968 normalisation, this progressive law remained a dead letter. The only authorised cultural body, CSEMADOK, was tightly restricted. The Hungarian Youth Union was abolished and 200 Hungarian schools were closed. A clandestine committee for the protection of the rights of Hungarian minorities in Czechoslovakia was founded in 1978. Its spokesman, Miklos Duray, signed Charter 77 as a founding member.

Let us look at some of the defining characteristics of the minority. At the 1991 census, 567,290 persons identified themselves as belonging to the Hungarian minority (10.8 percent) and 608,221 persons declared Hungarian as their native language (11.5 percent). Among the Hungarians, 64 percent are Catholics, 11.4 percent (20.5 percent in 1950) are Hungarian Reformed (Calvinists) and 2.2 percent Lutherans. The Hungarian minority lives along the Danube, in the valley of the Idonyi river, as far as Košice, in a thin band north of the 1920 border, some 345 km in length. Hungarians exceed 10 percent of the population in 523 townships and exceed 50 percent in 435 of them. The population is fairly rural (59 percent live in communities with fewer than 5,000 inhabitants. There are five cities with over 10,000 Hungarians, including Bratislava, Košice and Komarno. The main economic activity is agriculture. Unemployment is slightly above the Slovak average. There are two daily newspapers and limited programmes in Hungarian on Slovak radio and television. Cultural subsidies per head are lower for the minorities than for Slovaks.[66]

There are four political parties active in the Hungarian community. The largest, Co-existence, was founded in February 1990 as a broad party for all minorities (Poles, Ruthenians, etc.). It fought the 1990 elections in an alliance with the Hungarian Christian Democratic Movement, winning seats in both the Federal Parliament and the Slovak National Council. In 1992, it fought the elections in a broader alliance, also including the Hungarian People's Party, and again won representation in both Parliaments. Co-existence has observer status in the Liberal International. The Hungarian Christian Democratic Movement is a mainstream Christian Democrat Party that belongs to the EUCD. Founded in 1991, it is the second largest Hungarian party. The Independent Hungarian Initiative was founded in November 1989, but only became a fully independent party as the Hungarian Citizens' Party in January 1992. It ran on the VPN ticket in 1990 and served in the Slovak government between 1990-1992. In 1992, it did not meet the electoral threshold and has no seats, though it has some local councillors. It is a liberal party and also has observer status in the Liberal International. The Hungarian People's Party was founded in December 1991 and supports the rule of law, national reconciliation and a social market economy. Together, the Hungarian parties have close to 10 percent of the vote.[67]

	1990	*1992*
Hungarian Citizens' Party		2.29
Co-existence		
Hungarian Christian	8.66	7.42
Democrat Movement		
Hungarian People's Party	-	-

Note: The braces show that in 1990 two and in 1992 three parties ran as a ticket/coalition. The HPP did not exist in 1990, hence the dashes and the HCP did not run in 1990.

The Hungarian parties consider that they are discriminated against in many fields: local autonomy, cultural autonomy, cultural subsidies, use of language, the boundaries of administrative districts, education (an increasing number of Hungarian minority children cannot obtain places in Hungarian schools) and the contentious issue of place names. They also complain that the Slovak constitution defines the state as a "national state of Slovaks," and declares that minorities may not "endanger the sovereignty and territorial integrity of the Slovak Republic." Are their fears real or exaggerated? The prevailing opinion among Slovaks certainly seems opposed to giving the minority more rights. Many Slovaks consider that the Hungarian minority has enough rights already. A poll has shown that 56 percent of Slovaks would wish to deport the Hungarian minority. This is hard to believe, unless one has experienced the atmosphere in Slovakia. The minority certainly faces no immediate danger, but the tension that undoubtedly exists represents a potential future source of conflict between Slovakia and Hungary, in addition to the issue of the dam. The minority parties supported the censure vote against Mečiar in early 1994. They supported the Moravčik coalition from the outside, on the basis of an eight-point agreement on issues such as schools, cultural subsidies, place names and administrative districts. Their role was contested in the 1994 election.

Political developments in both Hungary and Slovakia in the first half of 1994 led to an improved atmosphere in relations between the two states and deliberate "cooling off" in the various conflict areas and active mutual efforts to improve relations. This concerned not only the Gabčikovo-Nagymaros issue, which was in any case "on ice" before the ICJ, but also in regard to other matters of dispute, such as the rights of the Hungarian minority.

The nationalist governments in both countries were removed, though only temporarily in Slovakia. Attempts to play the nationalist card in the Hungarian election of May 1994 had little effect. The most nationalist parties --the MIEP of Istvan Czurka and the main outgoing government party, the MDF, were severely defeated. The new Slovak coalition that replaced the Mečiar government in the spring sought cooperation with the Hungarian parties and was indeed dependent on their votes in Parliament.

Following defections from the HZDS in reaction to Mr. Mečiar's authoritarian style of leadership and policy divergences over economic policy, the HZDS-SNS coalition became a minority by early 1994. The confrontational style of the government, its intolerance and Slovakia's poor international image--which weakened its hand on key issues such as Gabčikovo and membership of the Council of Europe--led President Kovacs to join in attacks on the government. This was decisive in bringing together a coalition in Parliament to defeat the Cabinet on a motion of no-confidence. A four-party left/right coalition of the left-wing SDL, Christian Democratic KDH and two parties formed by former HZDS deputies (the Democratic Union of Slovakia, led by the new Premier Moravčik and the small National Democratic Party) was established. Apart from former Foreign Minister Moravčik, the coalition is dominated by SDL and KDH, who proved able to work reasonably well together. The coalition was supported in parliament by the main Hungarian parties (Co-existence and MKDM), on the basis of an eight-point platform of minority demands that the Cabinet has accepted and enacted. Clearly, the main cement of the coalition was a negative "stop

Mečiar" stance. However, it was able to agree on more: a new political atmosphere based on dialogue and consensus; a new economic policy and a commitment to improving relations with Slovakia's "near abroad": the Czech Republic, Hungary, Romania (with its sizable Hungarian minority) and Poland.

In Hungary, it had long been clear that the outgoing MDF-led coalition would probably be unable to win enough support in the election set for May 1994 to continue in office in its existing form. Premier Antall was losing popularity. After his death in late 1993, the position of the MDF became even weaker. Its coalition partner, the Smallholders, had suffered continuing internal rifts and splits. The only real question was which alternative coalition would emerge. In 1992 and 1993, the Young Democrats (FIDESZ) took the lead in the opinion polls. The SDS faced serious difficulties. Slowly, the MSZP (ex-communists) came up in the polls and by early 1994 was in the lead and was accredited with over 30 percent when the campaign began. Violent MDF attacks on the MSZP in the government-controlled media seemed to have had no deterrent effect on the determination of the electorate to defeat the MDF and to entrust the MSZP with power.

In the first round, the MSZP obtained a decisive breakthrough, with 32.96 percent, followed by the Free Democrats with 19.76 percent, slightly below their 1990 results. MDF was in a poor third place, with only 11.73 percent of the vote. FIDESZ won a mere 7.0 percent, falling behind the Christian Democrats, who actually made small gains. The Smallholders won 8.35 percent. The outgoing coalition in all obtained only 28.64 percent, less than the MSZP on its own. The MSZP adopted a very moderate position and sought to form a coalition with the Free Democrats, even if the MSZP were to win an absolute majority. The key issue in the second round in the 174 (out of 176 seats) where no candidate won 50 percent in the first round, was whether the MSZP should be entrusted with an absolute majority. That the MSZP would lead the government was no longer in doubt, but the Free Democrats attempted to mobilise voters to prevent an MSZP absolute majority. The electoral system, with its three-way contests, made this impossible. In the end, the MSZP won 209 seats, the SDS 70, MDF 37, Smallholders 26, Christian Democrats 22, FIDESZ 20 and Others 2. Thus, the MSZP won a working absolute majority. It formed a coalition with the SDS, with MSZP leader Gulya Horn as Prime Minister. A key policy goal of the new coalition was to improve relations with Hungary's near neighbours, including Slovakia. Otherwise, there was continuity in foreign policy goals.[68]

The four-party Moravčik coalition in Slovakia was committed to improving relations with Hungary, finding practical solutions to the interim water management problems in the old Danube and, if possible, concluding a basic treaty with Hungary, confirming borders and resolving the problem of minority rights. The visit of Prime Minister Horn to Bratislava did contribute to improving the climate and did set in motion expert water management discussions, but did not lead to any break through on the dam or on the position of the Hungarian minority. In the run-up to the Slovak election, no Slovak parties could afford to be seen to compromise too much with Hungary on either issue, nor equally could the new MSZP-SDS coalition accept the Slovak view on the rights of the Hungarian minority--the Slovaks' only wish to consider individual rights and not collective rights--or withdraw the dam case from the ICJ.

The coalition failed to win re-election. The left coalition lost heavily. Mr. Mečiar's HZDS emerged with 35 percent, only slightly below the 1992 result. Together with his SNS allies and the new Workers' Party, Mr. Mečiar formed a majority coalition.[69] This new government was less inclined to cooperation with Hungary.

The Historic Treaty of Friendship and Cooperation, the so-called Basic Agreement between Hungary and Slovakia, was signed by Premiers Horn and Mečiar on March 19, 1995 as part of the Paris Conference. This agreement was the belated fruit of a short period of more positive relations between the two countries, initiated by the Horn and Moravčik governments during 1994, which was greatly supported and encouraged by the international community, which brought pressure to bear on them to improve their relations and resolve outstanding bilateral differences. The agreement dealt with the inviolability of frontiers and mutual consent not to raise frontier claims in the future. There were significant and positive commitments on the status of minorities. Minority rights were designated as fundamental rights for the first time.

The Gabčikovo-Nagymaros issue was not touched in the treaty. Though there were political and technical discussions on the matter, no agreement was reached and both sides are looking to the ICJ ruling, which is due in late 1996.

The period of better relations was very short-lived and barely lasted beyond the signature of the agreement, under the international spotlight. The Hungarian Foreign Minister gave his gloss on the agreement by statement that even now "border change by peaceful means, through negotiations" remained possible under the treaty. On the other hand, the Chairman of the SNS, a junior coalition partner in Bratislava described the treaty as "unfortunate."

The treaty was ratified by the Hungarian Parliament on June 13, 1995 by 244 votes to 49, with 53 abstentions. So far, it has not been ratified by Slovakia and therefore is not in force. Furthermore, a draconian nationalist language law adopted in Slovakia in November 1995 has worsened the climate between Budapest and Bratislava.[70]

For its part, the Hungarian government has demolished the anyway incomplete works at Nagymaros and returned the Danube to its original bed in this stretch. This decision was hotly contested inside Hungary. Supporters argued that it was environmentally valuable in relation to ground water and irrigation problems and that it conformed to a long-held intention, expressed in numerous parliamentary resolutions. Opponents, including perhaps ironically, the Danube Circle, on the other hand, argued that this unilateral Hungarian decision could weaken Hungary's case before the ICJ and was in any case not environmentally justified.

Notes

1. George Schöpflin, *Politics in Eastern Europe*, Oxford: Blackwell, 1993, pp. 131-137 and 159-164 explores these issues.

2. Ibid., pp. 164-166.

3. Etienne Decaux, *La Conférence sur la Sécurité et la Coopération en Europe (CSCE)*, Paris: Presses Universitaires de France, 1992, pp. 12-13.

4. Texts of the Final Act published in A. Bloed, *From Helsinki to Vienna: Basic Documents of the Helsinki Process*, Dordrecht: Nijhoff, 1990.

5. M. Trémeau, "La dimension humaine de la CSCE", in Droit International et Droits de l'Homme, Cahiers du CEDIN, No. 5, p. 53.

6. Schöpflin, *Politics in Eastern Europe*, p. 179, refers to human rights as an "alternative mode" that is "a referent that transcended Marxist-Leninism."

7. K. Birnbaum and I. Peters, "The CSCE: a reassessment of its role in the 1980s", Review of International Studies (1990), Vol. 16, No. 4, p. 312.

8. On the Polish situation, Bodgan, *Histoire des Pays de l'Est*, Paris: Perrin, 1990, pp. 513-535.

9. "Negative Legitimation" was the proposition that the present situation was imperfect, but it was the least bad that was available at the given moment. As such, it disarmed external and internal critics. See Schöpflin, *Politics in Eastern Europe*, p. 216.

10. "Theses on Hope and Hopelessness," Survey 17, no. 3 (80), pp. 37-52.

11. "Pour un Plateforme Unique de l'Opposition" in *Politiques d'Aujourd'hui*, No. 3-4, 1977.

12. Adam Michnik, "Ce que nous voulons et ce que nous proposons" in *l'Alternative* no. 8/1981, pp. 5-14.

13. *Anti-politics*, London, Quartet: 1984.

14. J. Kis, *Politics in Hungary: For a Democratic Alternative*, Highland Lakes, New Jersey: Atlantic Research, 1989. He moved from pure moral "anti-politics" to the idea of a social contract, establishing "constitutional Communism."

70 Towards Democracy

15. Especially V. Havel, "The Power of the Powerless" in Keane, ed., *The Power of the Powerless: Citizens Against the State in Central-Eastern Europe*, London, Hutchinson: 1985, pp. 23-96.

16. Jan Patočka, *Essais Hérétiques*, Paris: Verder, 1982. He said of Charter 77: "Charter 77 is not a political act in the narrow sense, that is not a matter of competing with or interfering in the sphere of any function of political powers. Nor is Charter 77 an association or an organisation. It is based on personal morality."

17. "From Minority Status to Partnership: Hungarians in Czechoslovakia/Slovakia 1918-1992," Bratislava: Együtteles, 1993, p. 5.

18. Schöpflin, *Politics in Eastern Europe*, pp. 164-167 and 217-218.

19. Bogdan, *Histoire des Pays de l'Est*, p. 538 on Gorbachev and Central Europe.

20. Bogdan, *Histoire des Pays de l'Est*, pp. 556-557.

21. Schöpflin, *Politics in Eastern Europe*, p. 230.

22. Schöpflin, *Politics in Eastern Europe*, p. 231.

23. Interview with Mr. Droppa, General Secretary of the Danube Circle, August 1993.

Interview with Mr. Droppa and Tamas Fleischer, "Jaws on the Danube: Water Management, Regime Change and the Movement Against the Middle Danube Hydroelectric Dam" in International Journal of Urban and Regional Research, Vol. 17, No. 3 (1993), pp. 429-452, at pp. 433-435.

25. M. Bernhard, "Civil Society and Democratic Transition in East and Central Europe," in Political Science Quarterly, Summer 1993, pp. 307-326.

26. Bogdan, *Histoire des Pays de l'Est*, p. 557.

27. Janos Kis, *Politics in Hungary: For a Democratic Alternative*, Atlantic Research: High Lakes, 1989, and Schöpflin, *Politics in Eastern Europe*, p. 209.

28. Rupnik, *The Other Europe*, pp. 159-160.

29. Janusz Bugaski and Maxine Pollack, *East European Fault Lines: Dissent, Opposition, and Social Activism*, Boulder: Westview, 1989, pp. 212-214.

30. On Party formation, see Bogdan, *Histoire des Pays de l'Est*, pp. 559-560 and 577-578.

31. On Kadar's resignation, Bogdan, *Histoire des Pays de l'Est*, p. 559.

32. On nationalism, see Schöpflin, *Politics in Eastern Europe*, p. 279; for the conflict with Romania, pp. 543-546; and with Czechoslovakia, pp. 546-547.

33. For an account of these events, see Bogdan, *Histoire des Pays de l'Est*, pp. 577-588.

34. Bogdan, *Histoire des Pays de l'Est*, p. 580, on the new HSP.

35. Bogdan, *Histoire des Pays de l'Est*, p. 581.

36. A. Körösenyi, "Hungary" in Electoral Studies, Special Issue Elections in Eastern Europe, Vol. 9, No. 4 (1990).

37. On the election, see ibid.

38. On the parties, see Körösenyi, "Hungary," pp. 338-339 and 343-344 and footnote 7.

39. J. Pataki, "The role of the Smallholders' Party in Hungary," RFE Research Report No. 1/4, April 3, 1992.

40. Results, Körösenyi, pp. 342 and 343.

41. Pataki, "The role of the Smallholders' Party in Hungary."

42. On the Czurka split, see Laszlo Maracz, "Politieke Ontwikkelingen" in Het Nieuwe Hongarije in Oost-Europa Verknemingen No. 2, 128, July/August 1993.

43. Schöpflin, *Politics in Eastern Europe*, pp. 214-215.

44. Schöpflin, *Politics in Eastern Europe*, p. 159.

45. V.V. Kusin, *From Dubček to Charter 77: Czechoslovakia 1968-78*, Edinburgh, Q Press: 1978.

46. J. Valenta, *The Soviet Intervention in Czechoslovakia 1968 - Anatomy of a Decision*, updated edition, Baltimore: John Hopkins University Press, 1991, pp. 203-204.

47. For an account of developments in 1989, see Bogdan, *Histoire des Pays de l'Est*, pp. 589-594.

48. First aired in a BBC documentary. See also Valenta, *Soviet Intervention in Czechoslovakia - 1968*, p. 208, which refers to KGB efforts to remove Jakeš.

49. Timothy Garton Ash gives a detailed, insightful and colourful first-hand account of the role of OF in his *We the People*, Granta, 1990.

50. Interview with Jiri Boguzak, Head of the Expert Commission in Lidove Noviny on April 23, 1990.

51. G. Wightman, "Czechoslovakia," in Electoral Studies, Special Edition, pp. 319-326, at p. 320 on the electoral system.

52. On the parties and the campaign, see Wightman, pp. 321-322.

53. V. Havel interviewed in Respekt, April 24, 1990.

54. Results in Wightman, "Czechoslovakia," pp. 323-324.

55. Interview with Mr. Pštroš, advisor to OF, August 17, 1990.

56. Interview with Mr. Pštroš, then advisor to President Havel, on June 1, 1992, on these constitutional problems.

57. S. Kirschbaum, "Les Slovaques et le Droit des Peuples à Disposer d'Eux-Mêmes: à la Recherche d'une Solution" in Liebich and Roszler, eds. *L'Europe Centrale et ses Minorités: Vers une Solution Européenne*, Paris: Presses Universitaires de France, 1993, pp. 83-102, on the elections, p. 100.

58. For the chronology of the process, see Kirschbaum, "Les Slovaques et le Droit des Peuples à Disposer d'Eux-Mêmes," pp. 89-100.

59. Cited in Slovensky Narod, 29/1990, December 1, 1990.

60. Concepts explained by Jozef Markus, Chairman of the Matica Slovenska, in Slovensky Narod, 30/1991, July 18, 1991.

61. Kirschbaum, "Les Slovaques et le Droit des Peuples à Disposer d'Eux-Mêmes," p. 96 and interview with Deputy Speaker of the Slovak National Council, Mr. Jozef Prokeš (SNS) on September 3, 1993.

62. Kirschbaum, "Les Slovaques et le Droit des Peuples à Disposer d'Eux-Mêmes," p. 102.

63. Interviews with Mr. Prokeš (SNS) and Transport Minister Hofbauer (HZDS) in Bratislava, September 3, 1993.

64. "From Minority Status to Partnership: Hungarians in Czechoslovakia/Slovakia 1918-1992," published by Co-existence, Bratislava, 1993, p. 9.

65. Data from "From Minority Status to Partnership."

66. Data from "From Minority Status to Partnership."

67. "Hungarians in Slovakia," Information Bulletin, September 1992, p. 10.

68. See J. Fitzmaurice, "The Hungarian Election of 1994," Electoral Studies, Vol. 14, N° 1, 1995.

69. See J. Fitzmaurice, "The Slovak Election of September 1994," Electoral Studies, Vol. 14, No. 2, 1995.

70. Kissings Record of World Events, News Digest for March 1995, 40467.

5

The Dam or the Rise Before the Fall?

The idea of harnessing and controlling the River Danube is not new. The Danube as it was when the Gabčikovo-Nagymaros project began was far from being in its natural state. It had already been subject to considerable human intervention, both above and below the middle reach, where the dam system was to be constructed.

Yet Gabčikovo-Nagymaros system was on a scale beyond previous interventions and was considered by its critics as both unnecessary and excessive in terms of impact on the river and the surrounding environment. For its supporters, it was and is an environmentally justified project, bringing major economic advantages to the whole region. Inevitably, in this region, the project became invested with nationalist and political overtones that took the debate beyond purely rational cost benefit considerations on both sides and ultimately led to the internationalisation of the issue. It became a symbol, where rational argument was often used by both sides merely as a prop for their entrenched viewpoints. For the Hungarian ecologists and dissidents, the dam became a rallying point, a symbol of the communist regime with its obsession with economic growth by industrialisation and its ideological materialism expressed through control of nature. For the Slovaks, it became their project, to be defended against the hostility (after 1989) of both Prague and Budapest. For the Slovak nationalists, supporting the project was an act of political and cultural self-definition. As it were, with apologies to Derrida, by constructing the dam, the Slovaks have constructed themselves.

As we shall see, the search to control or tame the Danube, both to improve and extend its navigability and to prevent periodic catastrophic flooding, has been a recurrent concern. The idea of harnessing the Danube to generate power is not quite new either, with projects dating back at least to the early years of the twentieth century. The earliest records of serious floods on the Danube date back to the thirteenth century. Floods are recorded in

1445, 1501 (the most serious to date), 1721, 1787, 1876 and 1884. The earliest dykes were erected in 1426 and systematic flood protection measures were instituted in the seventeenth century, culminating in the period after 1850. River control, drainage channels and pumping stations were then added to the armoury of flood protection, but not with complete success as the devastating floods of 1954 in Hungary and those of 1965 in Slovakia showed.[1]

Nor is the idea of controlling the Danube to improve navigation new,[2] Apart from the Iron Gates area, the middle reaches in the so-called inland island between Bratislava and the bend remained the worst navigable area. Linking up the Rhine-Main-Danube rivers is an ancient goal that dates from as far back as the reign of the Emperor Charlemagne. The great Hungarian scientist and politician Count Szechenyi produced an extensive project for regulation works on the Danube in his essay "Regulaciones."[3] After the First World War, the International Danube Commission was calling for measures to improve navigation. It should not be forgotten that in medieval times and later, the Danube had no established main channel in this reach. As an early map of 1594 shows, it meandered through a series of channels, which themselves shifted.[4] It only developed in a main channel, in itself artificial, from the mid-nineteenth century.

The first projects for harnessing the Danube for hydro-electric power date from the later years of the last century. Proposals were made by Engineer Lafranconi in 1880, Dr. Fischer-Reinan in 1915 and Dr. Holeček in 1921, among others.[5] The Imperial government considered a plan in 1910.[6] At the peace conference in 1919, the new Czechoslovak State argued for and obtained the Danube frontier and a small toehold on the south bank, near Bratislava. It was less successful in emulating the French control over its border river, the Rhine in Alsace. The Treaty of Trianon in 1920 did not accredit Czechoslovak claims to unilateral rights to "utilise hydro-electric resources" of the Danube and Morava rivers.[7] This fact notwithstanding, the Czech government regarded, by interpretation, the very limited Article 290 of the Treaty as adequate grounding of its rights: "According to Article 290 of the Peace Treaty of Trianon, the Czechoslovak Republic is possessor of the exclusive right to utilise the hydro-electric power of border rivers under the supervision of the International Danube Commission."[8]

It can also be argued that Czechoslovak land reforms in the 1920s and measures after the Second World War sought to de-Hungarianise the Danube's northern bank which, coupled with its border rectification demands at the Paris Peace Conference in 1946, were aimed at establishing this control.[9] Moves in the inter-war period to rectify the Trianon border in

Hungary's favour, though seriously discussed even within the Czechoslovak government, were never realised.[10] The 1947 Paris Peace Treaty mainly confirmed the Trianon border but crucially added three villages on the south bank of the Danube, including Cunovo.[11]

For Hungary, the punitive Trianon Treaty had meant the loss of some 94.5 percent of its hydro-electric potential that had been located in areas ceded the new successor states (Czechoslovakia, Yugoslavia and to an expanded Romania).[12] Post-Trianon Hungary's absolute hydro-electric production potential was reduced to 7.5 billion kWh, of which the realistic upper limit is about 2 billion kWh of production. Of this, perhaps only half is economically viable, with 80 percent produced on the Danube and a mere 15 percent by the Tisza, Hungary's second largest river.[13] For Hungary between the wars as now, the problem was that its main hydro-electric resources lay in border rivers, with all the political complications that this entailed. This meant cooperation with neighbours. Thus, in 1935, the Hungarian Transport Minister Bornemisza put forward the first plan for a joint project on the Danube.

After the Second World War, discussion about national energy policy and with it, the role of hydro-electric power, gathered pace in each country. On both sides, there were battles between what observers such as Janos Vargha of the Danube Circle called the Water Management or Cement lobby and other interests. Indeed, the Hungarian economist Tamas Fleischer has analysed the whole process in terms of phases of conflict between "water management" and other political, social and economic forces.[14] This view is however not readily accepted in Slovakia. The long gestation period of the project almost thirty years from the late 1940s until the signature of the Treaty on September 16, 1977--shows that the water management interests and others who supported the dam project were far from having things their way. It took, in fact, a favourable combination of external circumstances to enable the project to be pushed through in both countries.

Hungary established a hydro-electric power agency in 1945 under the influential Professor Emil Mosonyi, and a first conference to discuss post-war energy needs was held in 1946. Initially, plans focused on dams on the Tisza river and especially at Tisza Lök, but the Danube around Nagymaros (Bös) area was also mentioned. Further conferences were held in 1952 and 1954. The 1954 conference examined the National General Plan for Water Management, which already included the concept of a power dam in the Visegrad area, to be jointly constructed with the Czechoslovaks.[15] In the meantime, Professor Mosonyi had suggested making contact with the Czech authorities to examine a joint power project along the Danube, as early as October 1950, during a meeting of the Hungarian Academy of Sciences. Similar plans were emerging on the Czechoslovakian side, and the first discussions between the two parties took place in 1952.

In the first phase, the discussions considered numerous and varied approaches and proceeded with little urgency or sense of direction. Indeed, at this stage, the main objective seems to have been more navigation and flood control than the energy considerations that were later to become of such central significance.[16] The technical experts and water management groups in the two countries came together in joint planning committees and soon reached preliminary agreement on the principle of a Danube dam scheme. At this point, the matter was not ripe for a decision at political level. Already at this early stage, the political scepticism came in the first place from the Hungarians. Prime Minister Gerö rejected a pre-cooked plan agreed on by the experts of the two countries. He also rejected, on economic and environmental grounds, the proposal for a side channel on the Slovak side. Despite this set-back, planning continued in both countries and in joint committees. The Czechs looked at no less than 13 variants in the border stretch, involving both river options and auxiliary land models.[17]

A number of political and economic factors militated against the project at this stage. Apart from the reticence that we have already noted in Hungary, the Czechs were not enthusiastic about diverting investment into this essentially Slovak Danube project, preferring to develop hydro-electric power on the Vlatava river in the Czech lands.[18] As so often, there was in this an element of conflict between the Czech and Slovak leadership. However, the most important obstacle was pragmatic: a serious scepticism about the economic viability of the project. In any case, it was difficult in increasingly planned economies to make objective market assessments of energy demand and costs/benefits of the project. There was here a conflict between the energy lobby and the water management lobbies.[19] The then applicable energy prices and subsidies for coal, Soviet gas and oil as well as the nuclear programmes were set in such a way that the hydro-electric dam scheme with its heavy up-front investment was seen as not being viable.[20] Externalities in the production of other polluting energies were not adequately included in relative cost calculations. In order to carry the day in this debate, the planners were obliged to postulate a demand for energy that had little firm basis and rejig their plans to maximise energy production, with accordingly inadequate concern for environmental consequences. This explains the continued emphasis on auxiliary side-canal models in preference to a river model.

There was also between 1962 and 1977 a complex redefinition of the project as a multi-purpose project, permitting a more favourable reallocation of costs. Thus, in 1962, energy production had to carry a hypothetical 90 percent of costs, against 10 percent for other (mostly navigation) benefits. By 1977, this calculation was radically rebalanced--energy at 60 percent, navigation 16 percent, water management 11 percent and infrastructure 14 percent--without any fundamental change in the actual scheme.[21] Energy production from the dam accordingly became more apparently competitive.

During the gestation period, numerous competitive variants were examined, over 400 environmental studies were commissioned, a regional impact study was set in motion and investment studies were undertaken. However, these various analyses remained relatively inconclusive, though in 1958 the Joint Hungarian-Czechoslovak Committee did recommend a scheme with two dams and a side channel. Thus, on October 7, 1958, a Joint Protocol was signed in Prague.

A number of cumulative factors intervened to provide a renewed and ultimately decisive political impetus to the project, leading to the signature of the Treaty in 1977. In the aftermath of serious floods--in Hungary in 1954, when 33,000 hectares were affected, and in Czechoslovakia (at Patince and Čičov) in 1965, when 100,000 hectares were flooded in 65 local authorities, leading to the evacuation of 65,000 people--the issue of more effective flood control measures was again raised.[22] The two states could only finance these extensive works if linked with energy production. There was a gradual awareness that the building of dams (28 in Germany and 9 in Austria) had reduced the transport of Alpine gravel. As a result, the faster flowing river was flushing out its bottom ground and deepening its bed below Bratislava, causing worse navigation conditions and a sinking of the ground water table, creating desertification.[23] Action was clearly needed.

Navigation conditions were clearly inadequate, and the Danube Commission had long been arguing for measures to improve the situation, as reliable navigation conditions only exist in this section for less than 160 days a year.[24] Dredging in the main channel had not resolved the problem. The special authority under the Danube Convention of 1948 (Annexe II) that was envisaged for the Gabčikovo-Gönyü section, similar to those in the Danube Delta and Iron Gates sections, was never established, although the riparian states drew up a proposal to that effect.[25] As the Rhine-Main-Danube Canal, under construction since 1921, neared completion (it finally opened in 1992), the bottleneck in this border section became even more serious.[26] More radical measures were needed.

The onset of the energy crisis, following massive world oil price increases by OPEC producers, altered the overall economic context. In the first place, it soon became clear that the socialist bloc was indeed affected by these price movements, a fact that Marxist economics had previously denied. Soviet oil prices were moving upwards. Energy economics were turned upside down. Relative prices now appeared in a different light: the hydro-electric option looked a good deal more favourable. It offered stable indigenous supply; it was safe and available. Once in place, cost of production would be stable. The impact of the energy crisis on western economies, with lower growth rates and hence lower import demand and the search for alternatives to imported oil also had implications for the central European economies. Creation of surplus hydro-electricity for export, especially for hard currency, now seemed a sensible economic strategy.[27]

Domestic political developments in both countries also contributed to creating a more favourable political climate for the project. After 1968, the Czechoslovak leadership became more Slovak-dominated and political decision-making, including investment decisions, became more receptive to Slovak interests. Indeed, the dam project became a unique example of a major Slovak interest becoming a Czechoslovak national interest. In Hungary, there was some internal tightening up and even back-tracking on reform in the 1974-1977 period, creating a climate in which the difficult internal expert and political debate on the project could be ended. This led, in 1975, to the leadership taking a decision of principle in favour of the project.[28]

Nor were the international factors entirely absent. As we have seen, there was discreet pressure from the Danube Commission. As early as 1955, there had been some initial COMECON interest in the Danube schemes. In 1963, the initial draft plans were ratified by COMECON's Permanent Committee on Electrical Energy Affairs and Agriculture.[29] The project was seen as an important element in COMECON economic integration in the Danube region. There was also Soviet political pressure to improve navigation on the Danube for military purposes.[30]

The combination of these pressures and the gradual maturation of the planning for the project eventually led to the signature of the treaty in Budapest on September 16, 1977 by Premiers Lazar for Hungary and Bilak for Czechoslovakia, following final agreement between the party leaders Janos Kadar and Gustav Husak on September 15, 1977. Instruments of ratification were exchanged on June 30, 1978 and the treaty then accordingly entered force on that date.

Let us now turn to look at this Treaty and the main characteristics of the Gabčikovo-Nagymaros project. The Treaty[31] is actually quite short and general, leaving many issues of detail to be determined by a joint contractual plan for the construction, by operating procedures agreed jointly and with general coordination being provided by government delegates from the two governments at both construction and operation phases. In all, the Treaty has 13 chapters and 28 articles. It established: the basic framework of the project and the key guiding principles; joint financing of the investment and joint ownership of the works; equal benefit from the electricity generated; operation "as single coordinated unit" (in Article 10(1)) for all the works. It laid down what each country was to build under the Treaty and established the period 1986-1990 for their completion.

This contractual plan laid down that the Dunakiliti weir and reservoir, the power canal and the Gabčikovo dam were to be completed by 1986 and the Nagymaros dam by the end of 1989. The Treaty undertakes some very minor, technical border rectifications in the river and canals but leaves the basic principle laid down by the Trianon and Paris Treaties intact, namely that the border runs in the main navigation channel in what was to become the old bed of the Danube. The Joint Contractual Plan was to include a water balance to be agreed between the parties, determining the allocation of water between the Moson Danube arm, other branches, the old Danube, the power canal. The Treaty confirms the existing obligations of the parties in relation to navigation under the Belgrade Convention of 1948. Article 5 of the Treaty and ancillary agreements provided for the sharing of responsibility for the various works and established the construction schedule. The system of financing is not so much a system of joint financing as of co-financing which allocated responsibility for different sections of the project. As a result, the Treaty left open the possibility, later taken up by Hungary, to involve outside sources of finance and of sub-contracting, especially from Austria. Interestingly, the Treaty is authentic in Hungarian and Slovak (Article 28). There is no apparent mechanism for denouncing the Treaty and its provisions cannot be modified, other than by protocols agreed on by both parties.

What are the main characteristics of the project as originally agreed?[32]
1. a 240 million cubic metre reservoir upstream of the Dunakiliti weir, created by impounding water in the flood plain between strengthened levées, between river km. 1860-1842 in Hungarian and Czechoslovakian territory between Dunakiliti and Hrušov;
2. the Dunakiliti weir at river km 1842 in Hungarian territory to raise the water level to divert water into the navigable power canal and to release

20 m³/s into the Moson Danube, 100 m³/s into the branches along the old
Danube and 200 m³/s in the summer and 50 m³/s in the winter into the
old Danube and 2000-4000 m³/s into the navigational channel. The weir
would raise the water level to 131.10 m above Baltic Sea level. It was to
have seven openings each 24.5 m wide;

3. a 17 km long diversion and navigational canal, extending from the
    reservoir, 540 m wide at the reservoir, decreasing to 267 m and
    extending to 737 m in front of the power plant at Gabčikovo. Its depth
    varies from 7.3 m to 14.3 m. The lining of the dykes consists of 5.0 m
    of asphalt concrete and a second layer of 8 cm dense concrete. It would
    create a depth of 19 to 23 m for the turbines;

4. the Gabčikovo power plant was to be equipped with eight turbines in four
    blocks. These are vertical kaplan turbines with runners 9.3 m in diameter
    and with a maximum capacity of 90 mW each. The total installed
    capacity is 720 mW. Twin navigation locks 275 m long and 24 m wide
    are situated to the left side of the power station. The locks can be filled
    in 15 minutes. The outlet canal, 8.2 m long, carries the water back to the
    old Danube above Palkovičovo, providing a deep water navigation route
    downstream of Gabčikovo. There would also need to be river regulation
    measures down to Nagymaros;

5. a second dam at Nagymaros, near the Danube bend beyond Estergom, at
    river km 1696.25. This was to consist of a weir on the right side of the
    plant with seven openings each 24 m wide, with radial gates up to 8 m
    and valves 3.3 m in diameter. There were to be six turbines in three
    blocks with an installed capacity of 158 Mw, much less than Gabčikovo,
    linked to both Slovak and Hungarian grids. On the left bank, there were
    to be two navigational locks 4 m wide and 275 m long. A road would
    run across the weir. There would be a lowering of the river bed by 80
    cm in a 40 km section below Nagymaros. The goal of the Nagymaros
    dam was to raise the water level to facilitate the passage of flood waves,
    to exploit differences in water levels for power generation by continuous
    operation and to improve navigation.

Construction work began in 1978, but the debate about the project was
not stilled. It continued among technicians and experts, though it was mostly
confined to matters of detail and did not apparently contest the political
decision to proceed or question the energy policy imperatives that the oil crisis
had now made the driving force behind the project. However, contracting
rates of economic growth and expanding debt burden in both countries raised
serious question-marks about their capacity to shoulder such a massive

investment burden. These financial considerations led to a renewed and more serious debate about the future of the project, especially in Hungary, which in 1982 demanded variously suspension, cancellation and rescheduling of the construction to extend it by ten years. Work had proceeded faster in Slovakia, where there was certainly no readiness to contemplate cancellation. Finally, a compromise was reached and included in a protocol to the 1977 Treaty, signed on October 10, 1983, following a period of suspension of work on both sides. The compromise extended the finalisation of the project by four years down to 1994.[33] Even at this stage, Hungary was less committed than Slovakia.

Certainly, the investment sums involved were massive. For Czechoslovakia, it involved 18.4 billion Czechoslovak crowns, with 2 billion Czechoslovak crowns at annually peak periods. Hungarian investment flow requirements were considerably less during this initial phase, as its construction proceeded more slowly. Naturally, ultimately it would have to meet an equivalent burden. These figures are hard to assess in comparative terms.[34] However, Hungary was obliged to agree to a $255 million compensation for Austrian firms covering work completed at Nagymaros and for breaches of contract in 1990.

Hungary had in the meantime been looking for a co-financing partner, which could only be in the west. Its neutral neighbour, Austria, was an obvious choice. Indeed, the Austrian energy, water management and construction industries had their own reasons to be interested in the Gabčikovo-Nagymaros dam.[35] Nine dams had already been built on the Danube; there was room for no more in Austria. An earlier cooperative project with Czechoslovakia for a dam at Wolfsberg had been abandoned in the late 1950s for financial and environmental reasons. Large-scale energy projects on or near the Danube were meeting solid political resistance in Austria. Following a national referendum, the completed Zwentendorf nuclear power station had been abandoned in 1978,[36] leaving Austria without a nuclear option. Indeed, an attempt to reopen the issue under the "small" Social-Liberal coalition in 1985 failed to achieve the necessary two-thirds majority in the Nationalrat.[37] A conventional power station planned for Hainburg on the Danube in an area of natural beauty near the Czechoslovak border led to massive protests in December 1984 and was abandoned by the SPÖ-FPÖ coalition. The writing was on the wall. By 1983, a Green party was already emerging and won enough support to enter Parliament in 1986. The FPÖ sought a green mantle and its 1985 programme took up an anti-nuclear and environmentalist stance. The other parties, despite their close links with the essentially pro-nuclear and pro-Hainburg social partnership organisations (employers, trade unions) were increasingly obliged to follow suit.[38]

Arrangements were therefore reached for Austrian construction firms, and in particular Donaukraft AG, to build the Dunakiliti weir and the Nagymaros dam, when its postponement ended in 1988.[39] The Donaukraft AG became the principle undertaking with numerous other Austrian sub-contractors. This required Austrian financing. While there was no formal treaty between the two states (this had been initially envisaged), the Austrian government was involved in several ways. Chancellor Vranitzky and Prime Minister Nemeth reached a political agreement on the concept of continuing Austrian support. The over 5.8 billion Austrian schilling loans which financed the work undertaken by Austrian firms involved and which would be repaid by electricity deliveries between 1996 and 2010 (91.2 ThWh per year - 66 percent of Hungary's share) were provided by publicly-owned Austrian banks such as the Credit Anstalt and the Länderbanken. Furthermore, in 1985, the Austrian Parliament specially amended the Energie-Anleihe Gesetz (Energy Loan Act), which authorised the Finance Minister to accord state loan guarantees where Austrian firms are involved in energy-related construction projects abroad and where loans are given against repayment in electricity. This fitted exactly the case of the Gabčikovo-Nagymaros dam.[40]

Austria is still insisting on repayment of the loans and has already in place the technical arrangements to receive its share of the electricity from 1996. Later attempts by private Austrian financiers, such as the former Austrian Finance Minister Hannes Androsch (SPÖ), and state banks to become involved in financing the works in Slovakia were opposed by the Austrian government. In early 1991, the Austrian government refused to give such guarantee of any loans, even though Austrian construction firms such as Keller AG were involved on the Slovak side. Austria had sought a balanced policy.[41] But in the view of the Austrian Green Party, it had not brought enough pressure to bear on Czechoslovakia against the project after 1989 and there is evidence that the Austrian Chancellor had initially considered supporting the Slovak position.[42] As the project became increasingly controversial,[43] the government decided--following pressure from the ÖVP, which was close to the Antall government in Hungary--that Austrian interests were better served by not supporting Slovakia.

Following these arrangements, in the mid 1980s the Hungarians resumed construction, and work at both Dunakiliti and Nagymaros began to seriously accelerate. The Austrian building firms made more rapid progress than expected. There was pressure, evident from late 1988, for a new zig-zag in Hungarian policy. Thus, despite growing internal opposition, the new reform cabinet under Premier Nemeth asked for a new revision of the Treaty to accelerate full completion. The probable reason was to create a fait accompli and so deprive the opposition of the issue. Furthermore, the Austrian subcontractors had almost completed the Dunakiliti Weir, and Nagymaros was advancing. It would be financially advantageous to bring the dam on stream earlier. Czechoslovakia, though as a result faced with some practical and financial difficulties, could in principle only welcome this Hungarian move as a belated more enthusiastic commitment to the project. The new protocol was signed in Budapest on February 6, 1989. This protocol deferred the completion date of Nagymaros by 15 months and Gabčikovo by 14 months. The project would have come on stream in 1992.

This was a misleading signal, the quiet before the storm. Opposition to the project had been building in Hungary especially since 1981 and was now about to reach a qualitatively new degree of politicisation; the dam, as it were, was about to burst.

Notes

1. On flooding of the Danube, see J. Liptak, *The River Danube of Europe*, Bratislava: NVK International, 1993, pp. 44-45.

2. Liptak, *The River Danube of Europe*, pp. 27-28 and 29-31.

3. Liptak, *The River Danube of Europe*, p. 51.

4. Map of Posniensis Comitatus, 1594 in Stav Vadotkov, 2 Obdobia 16 St.

5. Liptak, *The River Danube of Europe*, p. 79.

6. *Gabčikovo*, published by the MZR, Slovak Republic, Bratislava, 1993, 2.

7. On Czech post-war aims and strategy, see Peter Kien, "The Great Slovak Canal," Barrage, 1993, pp. 13-32.

8. Statement by Emil Zimmer, Head of the Water Management Department of the Czechoslovak Ministry of Public Works (1924), cited in Kien, "The Great Slovak Canal", p. 26.

9. Kien, "The Great Slovak Canal," p. 28.

10. Ignac Romsics "Edvard Beněs and the Czechoslovak-Hungarian Border," The New Hungarian Quarterly, Vol. XXXIII, No. 128, winter 1992, (94-106), pp. 105-6.

11. Kien, "The Great Slovak Canal," pp. 31-32.

12. A. Trummer and W. Lazsloffy, *Planned Water Management in Hungary*, Budapest, Vizugyi Kozlany: 1936, p. 333.

13. J. Vargha "Documents from the Gabčikovo-Nagymaros Barrage Systems History," Forum, 1989, pp. 3-4.

14. T. Fleischer "Jaws on the Danube: Water Management, Regime Change and the Movement Against the Middle Danube Hydro-electric Dam," in International Journal of Urban and Regional Research, Vol. 17, No. 3 (1993), pp. 429-443.

15. On the Hungarian proposals and plans, see Vargha, "Documents from the Gabčikovo-Nagymaros Barrage Systems History," 99. 4-23.

16. *Damming the Danube: What the Dam Builders Don't Want You to Know*, ed. J. Sibl, SZOPK/SRN, Bratislava, 1993, p. 4.

17. For an official Slovak view of this phase of the planning process, see *Système d'Aménagements Hydrauliques Gabčikovo-Nagymaros*, published by the Slovak Ministry of Transport, Post and Telecommunications and Public Works, Bratislava, January 1993, pp. 6-8.

18. Interview with Dr. Liska, Slovak Water Management (Vodohospodarska Vystaba), September 1993.

19. Kien, "The Great Slovak Canal," pp. 15-16.

20. Vargha, "Documents from the Gabčikovo-Nagymaros Barrage Systems History," pp. 28-29.

21. Vargha, "Documents from the Gabčikovo-Nagymaros Barrage Systems History," p. 30.

22. On the disasters of 1954 and 1965, see Liptak, *The River Danube of Europe*, p. 43.

23. *Système d'Aménagements Hydrauliques*, p. 5.

24. Liptak, *The River Danube of Europe*, pp. 31-32.

25. Liptak, *The River Danube of Europe*, p. 68.

26. On the Rhine-Main-Danube Canal, see Liptak, *The River Danube of Europe*, pp. 32-34.

27. On the energy debate and shift in opinion, see *Damming the Danube*, pp. 5-6.

28. On these internal political debates, see Fleischer, "Jaws on the Danube," p. 432.

29. Kien, "The Great Slovak Canal," on COMECON involvement, p. 34.

30. Kien, "The Great Slovak Canal," p. 33.

31. Treaty between the Hungarian People's Republic and the Czechoslovak Socialist Republic concerning the construction and operation of the Gabčikovo-Nagymaros system of locks, signed at Budapest on September 16, 1977. U.N. Treaty Series (translation), Vol. 1109, pp. 1-17134.

32. What follows derives from Liptak, *The River Danube of Europe*, pp. 81-88.

33. On this compromise, see *Systèmes d'Aménagements Hydrauliques*, pp. 9-10.

34. Czechoslovak figures provided by Dr. Liška. Useful data on cost is found in the Hardi Report (Expert Review for the (Hungarian) Council of Ministers on the ecological, environmental, technological, economic, international and legal issues of the Bös-Nagymaros Barrage System), September 1989, pp. 16-18.

35. Fleischer, "Jaws on the Danube," p. 435.

36. On Zwentendorf, see J. Fitzmaurice, *Austrian Politics and Society Today*, London, Macmillan: 1991, pp. 109-110.

37. A. Pelinka, *Die Kleine Koalition SPÖ-FPÖ 1983-86*, Vienna, Böhlau: 1993, pp. 44-45.

38. Fitzmaurice, *Austrian Politics and Society Today*, p. 111 and Pelinka, *Die Kleine Koalition*, pp. 42-43.

39. See *Umwelt Bericht*, (Slovakia, Hungary and Austria) Monogaro Environment Charter Consulting Organisation, Vienna-Bratislava, 1993, for information on Austrian involvement, p. 65f.

40. Information provided by Dr. Meister of the Bundesumweltsamt, Vienna.

41. Die Presse, February 2, 1991.

42. Interview with Mr. Noel, advisor to the Austrian Green Parliamentary Group, September 10, 1993.

43. J. Galambos, "Political Aspects of an Environmental Conflict: the Case of Gabčikovo-Nagymaros" in *Perspectives on Environmental Conflict and International Relations*, ed. J. Kakonen, London and New York, Pinter: 1992.

6

The Impact of the Fall of
Communism on the Dam

As we have seen, the decision to build the dam was ultimately taken for political reasons. The conflicts about the dam project that arose from the mid-1980s were also ultimately political, though important economic interests were also at stake. The technical debate of the early 1980s that was becoming increasingly critical of the project would not in itself, even in Hungary, have ever led to the abandonment of the project. Timing too was a crucial factor. Hungary was always more reticent and was building more slowly, so that by the time a serious critical debate began, far less of the works had actually been undertaken than in Slovakia. Had Hungary been closer to the Slovak rate of completion, pressure for cancellation would have been much weaker.

In Hungary, democratisation was proceeding more rapidly than construction. In Slovakia, the reverse was the case. The Prague regime remained hardline, Slovak-dominated and pro-dam until its sudden collapse in November 1989. By that time, Hungary had already taken many key decisions leading towards cancellation. On the other hand, construction in Slovakia was far advanced, up to 90 percent at Gabčikovo. This lack of parallelism and even reverse symmetry is an important factor in understanding the opposite stances taken by the two sides. As a result, as we have seen, the Gabčikovo-Nagymaros dam became a symbol in both countries, but a positive symbol in Slovakia and a negative one in Hungary.

Before looking at the chronology and analysis of the rise of opposition to the dams and the conflict between the two countries, let us first look systematically at the issues raised in the debate in favour of the dams and against them.

The project's main purpose and justification in the eyes of its promoters is energy production. They argue that hydro-electricity is safe, clean and relatively cheap energy, when compared with either nuclear energy or the continued use of coal-fired power stations.[1] In their argumentation lies an implicit and at times even explicit form of blackmail towards the west and in particular towards Austria and Germany: Do not expect us to renounce potentially dangerous nuclear installations near our western borders such as Bohunice unless we can develop the Gabčikovo-Nagymaros project.[2] They argue that 3.9 million tonnes of brown coal or 1.4 million tonnes of oil annually would be saved and equivalent pollution could thus be avoided.[3] The Slovak government argues that the production cost of 1 mWh of electricity is 311 Czech Crowns (KCŠ) for fossil power plants; 261 KCŠ for nuclear power plants and only 148 KCŠ for hydro-electric plants.[4] In addition, it is argued that the 4 billion kWh that the dams could produce would significantly improve the energy balance in both countries and reduce dependence on external energy sources.[5] Even so, it would produce no more than 10-15 percent of the expected Slovak electricity consumption of about 20 billion kWh per year. Hungarian protagonists of the dam--a small minority in that country--argue that Hungarian industrial development will need the additional electricity and that energy efficiency is not a real alternative.[6]

Opponents of the dam, many of whom do not in any case place the economic issue in the forefront of their case, also dispute this economic analysis on several grounds, both general and particular. Reputed economists and indeed the Hungarian government's Advisory Commission (Hardi Report) attacked the historic cost evaluation for both excluding very significant externalities and for under-estimating cost overruns.[7] The Hardi report also noted that the Hungarian Ministry of Environment and Water Management organisation were obliged to concede that the project, even in its original form, would not be profitable. Without Nagymaros, and with a greater flow of water in the old Danube, it would become less so.[8] Continuation and cancellation were only being weighed on a static investment cost basis. More radically, the Hardi report also argued for cancellation on the grounds of opportunity cost of the released resources.[9] Even more radical challenges have been made to the demand side of the equation. The original plans posited an energy shortage in 1992-1996 until nuclear plans would come on line. Beyond that period, coal and nuclear-generated electricity would meet the base load and Gabčikovo-Nagymaros would meet the peak load.[10] Actually, whatever policies are pursued, lower growth than predicted and energy economics will reduce energy consumption per unit of production as the ex-communist economies modernise and increase their productivity.[11] Beyond that, it is argued that the entire dam concept is based on a productivist ideology which encourages energy inefficiency, which is already 10-15 percent above west European levels. Instead, it is argued, resources should be devoted to a realistic energy-saving policy that could lead to savings of up to 30 percent by the year 2010.[12]

Much of the argumentation against the dam is based on non-economic and non-materialist concerns. Even the Hardi Committee states: "The continuation or cancellation of construction of the barrage system is not an economic issue. Up to this day, decisions that been made at the environmental-ecological and socio-political levels in power groups, and the fate of the hydro-electric station will continue to be decided on that level."[13] Indeed, for most of the opposition and for much Slovak opinion, the economic arguments are not of decisive relevance. The opposition would fight the project even if it could be convinced of its economic viability. Its arguments cover a very wide range of what are broadly environmental or cultural issues. They range from very general concerns about interference in nature and "gigantism" and the special cultural role of the Danube river, to more specific matters of ground water, natural environment, agriculture and fisheries in the area of the works and the safety of this construction itself. In an interesting analysis, the Hungarian lawyer Boldisar Nagy discusses this in terms of two opposed and conflicting paradigms. He sees the Hungarian position as post-modern, non-growth but preservation orientated. On the other hand, the Slovak approach is, he says, "dominated by a modernisation driver and growth-oriented." He sees a modern versus post-modern conflict.[14] It should be noted that these arguments were initially deployed against the original project, and were only reinforced by Variant C--the unilateral Slovak deviation of the Danube waters at Cunovo, which was seen, if anything, as even more radically anti-environmental. The Slovak view is that the effects of Variant C will "have a more limited effect on the Hungarian side and so they cannot be considered as significantly harmful."[15] This view is not accepted by Hungarian opinion.

These debates are extremely complex and, in many areas, cannot, at least as yet, be conclusively answered by reference to scientific or measurable evidence. That stricture goes equally for those who deny any deleterious effect on the environment as it does for those who seek to point to environmental improvements deriving from the project. This jury is still out on these contradictory scientific arguments.

Critics argue that there has not been an adequate environmental impact study. They point to the loss of 13,500 acres of near natural state land. Another key criticism relates to the impact on habitat and hence the threat to many plant and animal species living on the wetlands and floodplain forests.

Opponents point to the reduction of water levels in side arms. They underline the threat to the ground water levels and the impact of pollution on drinking water supplies for Budapest from both the Danube area and from the trans-Danubian mountain Karst water. Another major problem raised by critics is the potential change in the oxygen regime of the river water. It is argued that the impact of slower water flow and biological changes threaten entrophization, destroying the river's biological filtration capability; threaten water quality; and seriously affect agriculture near the river by desertification and fish stocks in the river. This represents an extreme simplification of a very complex scientific critique of the project that has been developed by bodies such as the Danube Circle and the World Wildlife Fund, but it underlines the main conclusion of these criticisms.

Slovak official statements and Hungarian supporters of the project regard these concerns, in most cases, as unjustified, at best exaggerated and at worst, tendentious. They do not accept that they are any less concerned about the environment than their critics. Indeed, they argue that the situation of the Danube before the project was far from perfect. Indeed, they even predict environmental improvements: "Given the precautions built into the project, Gabčikovo-Nagymaros will not cause an environmental catastrophe, but in fact will improve the present condition of the river. The environmental risks of building and using Gabčikovo-Nagymaros are smaller than expected," stated Dr. Binder, Director of the Slovak investment company, Vodahospodarska Vystaba.[16] Supporters argue that the quality of ground water has not and will not be reduced or polluted. Nor do they see any serious threat to Budapest water supplies. They also contend that the impoundment of water has stopped erosion of the bed and hence will prevent lowering of the ground water surface. Such impoundment also feeds the deeper aquifers and secures a steady supply of water to the Moson Danube. With appropriate measures in the side arms on the Hungarian side similar to those already implemented on the Slovak side, both the natural and environmental and water supply would both be safeguarded and in some cases improved.[17] They argue too that the threat of pollutants entering the water supply is merely theoretical.[18]

Some criticism has been directed at the solidity of the construction, to its imperviousness to seepage and dangers of flooding in Budapest and in agricultural areas adjacent to the construction.[19]   A recent accident in the Gabčikovo lock closed the channel for 38 days, renewing these concerns. These criticisms are rejected as unfounded and theoretical, especially in regard to the threat of flooding Budapest. Indeed, it is argued that the system will provide a much higher degree of protection against flooding than has hitherto been possible.

Improvement of navigation in the middle section of the Danube, in accordance with long-standing recommendations of the Danube Commission, is one of the most important arguments advanced in favour of the project. Indeed, some would argue that this has now become the key argument that has led to cooling off of western support for the environmental opposition, and determined the low-key western reaction to the introduction of Variant C. Equally, EC mediation efforts sought compromises that would not require the existing construction to be demolished, so maintaining these navigation improvements.[20]

For its supporters, the dams are seen as part of a wider process of developing inland waterways. It is pointed out that this middle section of the Danube was the last remaining bottleneck on the Danube. It is seen as part of the development of a Europe-wide river network, linked up with the Rhine, Main and Danube Canal and potentially with Danube-Oder-Elbe and Danube-Adriatic Canals.   These new interlinked waterway systems would, with modern container and RO-RO transport systems, make water transport highly competitive.[21]   There is, it is argued, considerable potential for transferring traffic to waterways. Currently, its share of international freight traffic is a mere 7.7 percent in eastern Europe, compared with 35.1 percent in western Europe.[22]   It also offers the lowest per km rates, when compared with other alternative modes of transport.   The Gabčikovo-Nagymaros dam can guarantee full navigability compared with the previous situation in which the river was not fully navigable for 200 days per year.

Opponents of the project put forward a more sceptical and balanced argumentation, without though denying that improved navigation on the Danube is desirable and will generate some increased traffic and lead to transfers from other more expensive and more polluting modes.[23] They argue that the increase in traffic will be limited and will not benefit the riparian states principally.   They consider that it can have perverse and negative consequences for the riparian states and that the Gabčikovo-Nagymaros dam project itself will not improve navigation.[24]   The Cousteau Report argues cogently that Gabčikovo-Nagymaros alone will not significantly improve navigation, that even a fuller programme of works will only lead to a small annual increase in traffic created or diverted (+1.8 million tons) and only a small increase in productivity of existing traffic flows. The only beneficiaries would be the CIS states, the collaboration between Austrian VAG and Slovak BAZ car producers, and the Voest steel industry in Austria, which could imperil the existence of the Slovak steel industry. It concludes on "the non-advantageous nature as far as navigation is concerned"[25] and proposes alternative works to improve navigation, which would produce some limited benefits.

Proponents of the dams see them as a potential catalyser of regional development in the reach between Vienna and Budapest, especially in relation to the Vienna-Győr-Bratislava triangle, which covers the most developed areas of both Hungary and Slovakia that could take advantage of their proximity to Austria, now an EU Member.

As we shall see in more detail, legal and political issues have also played a prominent part in the debate. Hungary argued that changed circumstances permitted it, in 1989, to terminate the 1977 treaty. Czechoslovakia denied this claim. For its part, Slovakia regards its implementation of Variant C as a justified response to that breach of law by Hungary, fully in line with the original purposes of the treaty, a claim denied in turn by Hungary. It is this complex of legal issues that has been referred to the International Court of Justice in the Hague.[26] (See Chapter 7).

For both sides, the dam issue has an important political dimension.[27] For both, it was a rallying symbol, positive for the Slovaks and negative for the Hungarians. For the Slovaks, the position was greatly complicated before 1992-1993 by the Federal link as the Czechs were, after 1989, less than totally committed to the project. This obliged the Slovaks to fight on two fronts. For both sides, the issue had implications for their "return to Europe." Both sides sought to develop and mobilise international alliances with the other country and more widely in Europe. Both sides sought to internationalise the issue in various fora: the Danube Commission, CSCE, the EU and in bilateral contacts with key regional powers such as Austria and Germany. In those contacts, both sides invoked issues of stability, navigation, energy supply cleaner energy and western values of respect for democratic principles and the rule of law.[28] Initially, Hungary enjoyed a better image in the west, but the Slovaks have been on a rapid learning curve and their presentation of their case has improved exponentially.

The opposition to the project that was eventually to lead to the serious conflict between Hungary and Slovakia built slowly. As we have seen, there was always a less wholehearted, more critical approach to the project in

Hungary than in Czechoslovakia. The conflict was made more complex by the involvement of both Austria on the margins and the Czechs who, after 1989, became separate independent actors that were caught in a dilemma between their substantive opposition to the project and the need not to aggravate the already fraught state of Czech-Slovak relations.[29]

Opposition built from the initial largely technical critiques into a political anti-system movement in Hungary, leading in 1989 to the decision to cancel the project. In response, Czechoslovakia was passive and immobile. There was virtually no opposition to the project there and certainly no willingness on the part of the regime to reconsider its position, for to do so would have been perceived as a serious defeat and loss of face in capitulating to demands similar to those that might be raised by its own underground dissidents. However, once Hungary actually moved towards cancellation, a complex three-way negotiation between Prague, Bratislava and Budapest developed.

From 1980 onwards, a number of Hungarian experts such as a railway engineer, a civil engineer, a hydrobiologist and researchers at the Scientific Institute of Water Management ventilated detailed professional criticisms of the project. However, these criticisms did not lead to a wider debate, nor lead the authorities to take any corrective action.[30] It took the action of one man, a biologist and journalist with Buvar (Diver), a nature protection monthly, to move the debate on. This man was Janos Vargha, who became interested in the issue in 1981, when he was alerted to the issue by people living near the works. As his investigations continued, he became shocked by the suppression of criticism, and by the lack of open debate that he found. Opposition and even constructive criticism was being ignored and the project steam-rollered through by fiat. His original report was suppressed. He then continued his research into the wider historical and political background and in November 1981 published a dramatic critique of the project in VALOSAG (a social sciences monthly). This coincided with some limited international criticism of the project and a temporary construction halt. Vargha was then asked to sit on an advisory committee by the Academy of Sciences.[31]

These developments pointed to a degree of uncertainty in the upper reaches of the leadership and indeed in the Academy of Sciences, a very official body and a pillar of the regime that was influencing some members of the Politburo.[32] A degree of space for debate was now opening up. One additional reason was competition for limited resources. Rival experts were encouraged by these hesitations to re-open old issues. The rivalry between the hitherto ascendent water management and the energy lobbies, especially coal and nuclear, revived. At this time, the project was delayed by four years by the 1983 protocol, and the search for external financing began. Vargha gave a minority opinion in the Advisory Committee, wrote underground articles and a public article in the HGU weekly on this additional protocol.[33] He was now coming to the view that the regime could not be moved by this kind of expert activity, but only by a broader, more political debate.[34] Indeed, as events were to show, the regime was leaning back to a harder line and would, in 1985, reconfirm the project at the highest level. In doing so, it rejected a growing body of technical and professional opposition, which was developing within official and semi-official bodies such as government economists, the Győr-Sopron County People's Supervisory Committee, the Hungarian Hydrological Society, the Association of Technical and Natural Sciences Societies, the National Environmental and Nature Protection Office, which now felt able to express their views openly.[35] Clearly, the policy could only be reversed at a political level. The time was ripe for a broader, more political campaign.

A number of different activists came together in what was to become the Dunakör (Danube Circle).[36] They were able to take advantage of the hesitant, two steps forward/one step back approach of the authorities. The negative opinions of small professional groups were not suppressed, but were ignored. The more dangerous negative opinion of the prestigious Academy of Sciences was actually banned. The project was continued, yet the debate was allowed to continue as well. Thus, on January 27, 1984, Janos Vargha was invited by the Embankment Club in Budapest to a debate with the Deputy Chairman of the Water Management authority. The Deputy Director withdrew at the last minute. Vargha spoke at the meeting and afterwards, 30-40 people continued the discussion and decided to launch a campaign.[37] Secret meetings were held in the now famous Fonduë Bar. Signatures were collected on petitions and information was circulated. Speakers were provided for meetings near the site and elsewhere in the north and west of Hungary and small demonstrations began to be organised. People in the Szentendre area, later to refound the Smallholders' Party, got in touch with Janos Vargha and then organised meetings and protests in their own locality, especially by farmers in local clubs. Even the local Communist Party took part.[38] For a short period in 1984, there was a quite open debate in progress until the Water Management succeed in imposing an "information blackout."[39] The government began to re-impose censorship restrictions. The response was the semi-underground newsletter of the Danube Circle and a broader petition campaign. Over 10,000 signatures were collected on a petition to parliament calling for postponement of the project and for new plans to be drawn up. The Danube

Circle became more structured and developed foreign links. It was refused registration and so remained "semi-clandestine" on the spurious grounds that there was already an official body responsible for coordinating environmental NGOs. In 1986 and 1987, the police took a tougher line, dispersing demonstrations and deporting foreign demonstrators. A 2,500 signature petition was presented on January 30, 1986, calling for a referendum, and a march in support was planned for February 8, 1986 but this was prevented by the police.[40]

The movement now faced a dilemma. Was it, as Janos Vargha preferred, a single issue environmental movement, or was it a broad political oppositional movement, attacking the regime on myriad front? This second broader concept took over, with the campaign for a referendum and with the participation of Hungarian intellectuals through advertising campaigns against the dam and against Austrian financial involvement that were published in the Austrian national newspaper, Die Presse, in April 1986.[41]

By 1988, the gradual liberalisation and reform process was in motion. In 1985, a few independents had been elected to Parliament. This hitherto moribund body began to awake, and these independents were prime movers in the summer of 1988 in calling for a new and open parliamentary debate on the project.[42] During the early autumn, pressure on Parliament against the dams was maintained: a joint Dunakör-World Wildlife Fund Conference on September 4, a mass demonstration of 30,000 people in front of the Parliament. It was in vain. The very severe pressure from the party was effective for almost a last time. With only four votes against, the project was again confirmed, with some limited environmental conditions: "The ecological risks have to be reduced a minimum and for this reason, both in the course of the investment and operation, ecological interests shall take priority over economic interests."[43]

Public opinion was far from satisfied by this all too familiar exercise of naked power in the old manner by the party. The campaign of demonstrations and collection of signatures continued and intensified. Over 140,000 signatures were presented to Parliament at the end of February 1989.[44]

In the meantime, the reformist movement was triumphing. In December 1988, the reformist Miklos Nemeth became Prime Minister. He needed to head off the movement and at all costs avoid a referendum that would, in the prevailing circumstances, have become a referendum on the regime itself and demonstrated its lack of legitimacy. He therefore needed to distance himself from the party and win time. In March 1989, he already began to hint at a shift in policy.[45] The Academy of Economic Sciences was asked to prepare an opinion, which later led to the Committee of Independent Experts, chaired by Professor Hardi, that contained several engineers, biologists, the international lawyer Laszlo Valki and Janos Vargha, which reported in September 1989.[46] In May 1989, Premier Nemeth made a very critical speech on the project in Parliament. On May 13, the Hungarian government decided on a moratorium on construction at Nagymaros, initially for two months, later extended.[47] This decision was conveyed to the Czechoslovak Prime Minister on May 24, together with the opinion of the Hungarian Academy of Sciences. The Hungarian side proposed further studies and joint analysis of the ecological risks arising from the operation of the dam system.

On June 2, 1989, the Hungarian Parliament approved the government decision and adopted resolutions setting up a Committee for further investigations "on the conditions and consequences of the construction."[48] At the same time, the government was authorised to enter into negotiations with the Czechs on any modifications to the treaty, necessitated by those new studies. Thus, the Hardi Committee was set up. Two expert conferences between the two countries in July and then in September reached no conclusions on the main issue, only on subsidiary questions about water quality. The Hungarians proposed various variants of suspension for three to five years and cancellation. The Czechoslovak side, in a note of August 1, 1989, protested against what it considered the illegal unilateral action of the Hungarians and on August 25, 1989 demanded compensation if the Hungarians did not complete Nagymaros. On August 31, 1989, the Czechoslovak side indicated for the first time not only that it rejected the Hungarian proposal but that it was studying the possibility of carrying out measures, on its own territory, to reduce the damage that it was suffering and to ensure an adequate flow of water to the Gabčikovo hydro-electric power station[49] in the event that Hungary maintained its suspension of the project. The Hungarian reply dated August 4, 1989 protested at this veiled threat as a violation of international law.

The die was now cast. On October 31, as the Hungarian reform process gathered speed, the Hungarian Parliament took note of the conclusions of the Hardi Report, which recommended cancellation of Nagymaros, the peak-time operation and the Dunakiliti weir. The resolution that was approved by parliament followed this recommendation, but significantly at this point stopped short of calling for dismantlement of the Nagymaros works. It also called for a reassessment of the ecological dangers of the Gabčikovo works and finally for a renegotiation of the 1977 treaty. These demands were transmitted on November 3 and 30, 1989, to which there was never a direct reply, no doubt due to the internal turmoil in Czechoslovakia.[50] By now, the basic battle lines were drawn and all the elements that were to figure in the conflict were on the table.

Abandoning, or at the very least deferring, the Nagymaros dam and demanding a serious ecological debate about Gabčikovo was now part of the political survival strategy of the Nemeth cabinet, just as the earlier acceleration decision had been intended to complete the dam before opposition could become even stronger. It had to head off the opposition and seize the initiative on this issue, which had become a symbolic totem, if it was to have any chance of surviving the transformation of Hungary into a democratic state. The cancellation decisions were part of that strategy. As we have seen, the arguments for and against the project are quite well balanced. In the end, following the analysis of Boldisar Nagy, it was a choice of paradigms. For opponents of the dam, even small ecological risks were not worth taking.[51] For the Water Management in both countries and the hardline Czechoslovak leadership, there was no reason to modify their position.

There, the situation rested, at a stand-off, when the communist regime in Czechoslovakia began to collapse after November 17, 1989. By the end of 1989, President Havel was in power. In Prague, his close ally, Jiri Dienstbier, was the new Foreign Minister in the reform cabinet of the moderate Slovak, Marian Čalfa. This raised hopes in Hungary that this would lead to a radical change of policy on Gabčikovo-Nagymaros in Prague, as Havel and other dissidents had always opposed the project from the underground. Yet, neither the new reform communist Hungarian leadership, nor later, the democratically elected MDF government, nor the new Czechoslovak government, devoted adequate political attention to the issue. It simply was not their first priority, which is understandable.[52] There was a serious failure on the Hungarian side to understand the complexity of the political situation in Czechoslovakia. Above all, the difficulty of the relationship between Czechs and Slovaks was not adequately taken into account by Hungarian policy makers.[53] Nor was it realised that, as a consequence, the Czech leadership had almost no room for manoeuvre on this matter. Compounding this error, the Hungarians took no new initiatives in the early summer of 1990, simply waiting for the expected change in Czechoslovakian policy. It was not realised that the Czech side, though certainly opposed to the project, was obliged to take account of Slovak sensitivities. The Czechs could not afford to open up a new area of contention with Slovakia at this point. Hungary therefore failed to develop any alternative strategy and certainly failed to realise that the earlier Czechoslovak threats of unilateral action remained a serious possibility which the Czechs would not be able or willing to restrain. At the same time, neither side was ready at this stage to submit the issue to international arbitration, fearing that its intransigent stance would not be accepted by any outside body.[54]

Against this background, a series of negotiations was initiated at different levels, conducted both by face to face high-level meetings, in joint committees, by experts and by diplomatic exchanges of aides-memoires and note-verbales which were to lead nowhere. Positions on both sides actually radicalised. The Hungarians moved to dismantle Nagymaros, though the Slovaks considered that under the 1977 treaty, denounced by Hungary, these works were joint property. The Slovaks moved to prepare to implement Variant C (diversion of most of the Danube waters into a navigation channel in Slovak territory. Much of the background to these radicalisations and unwillingness to compromise must be sought in the domestic political situation in each country. How did the Gabčikovo-Nagymaros issue play in the domestic politics of Hungary, Czechoslovakia and then in Slovakia, since from early 1992 Federal Czechoslovakia to all intents and purposes ceased to exist? What were the positions of the various political actors?

In the Czech Republic, leading dissidents such as Vaclav Havel and Jiri Dienstbier had opposed the project before 1989. This was one point on which both the Havel-Dienstbier wing of the OF and the Klaus wing agreed. Jiri Dienstbier, in his first visit to Budapest as Czechoslovak Foreign Minister on January 12, 1990, disassociated himself from the gigantomatic policies of the past but offered no more concrete proposals. This was perhaps a misleading signal.[55] Yet, after the "Wende" in 1989-1990, the key issue soon became Czech-Slovak relations, to which everything else had to be subordinated.

As we have seen in Chapter 4, these relations soon became extremely difficult. Havel, with his insistence on maintaining national unity within a Czechoslovak nation, came increasingly to be seen by the Slovaks, not as a President of both nations, but just as anti-Slovak as Czech Presidents Masaryk, Beneš or even Gottwald. His interventions in Slovak affairs such as the removal of Mečiar as Slovak Premier in April 1991 did little to alter that perception. It reminded people of the behaviour of the Czechoslovak central government in the late 1930s.[56] It made Havel unacceptable to the Slovaks as President after the 1992 elections. Against such a background, the views of Prague political leaders on Gabčikovo were unlikely to be accepted by Slovak opinion. Czech political leaders thus at first sought to back-pedal, stating an opposition of principle, coupled with such a degree of concessions to the Slovaks that it amounted in reality to abandoning decision-making on the issue to Bratislava. Despite the fact that the interim Federal Cabinet that held office from the 1992 elections until the ultimate break-up of Czechoslovakia in January 1993 was evenly divided over the construction halt, proposed by Hungary and the EC in October 1992, the Czech side in practice abdicated responsibility and tolerated the implementation of Variant C. Indeed, Federal Vice Premier Antonín Baudys put the position well when he said "the Czechoslovak Federal Government has de jure, but not de facto control over the project."[57]   His colleague, Czech Finance Minister Ivan Kočarnik was even more direct, saying that "Gabčikovo was not a Czech problem."[58]

On the side of the hill, the Slovak political scene had been turbulent since the collapse of Communism. The VPN (Public Against Violence) had always been weaker than the OF. It had not even won an absolute majority in 1990. It had been less liberal, less unitarian and less market-orientated. It had always been more nationalist.[59] In Slovakia, public support was attached to political leaders active in the Slovak government and not for "federal Slovaks." The removal of the popular Mečiar in April 1991 and his replacement by the Christian Democrat Čarnogursky was seen as in part manipulated from Prague and so rebounded against its Slovak beneficiaries. Mečiar then created a new political movement, designed as his own political vehicle. It was a clearly Slovak movement, but unlike the Slovak National Party, it was ambiguous about economic reform and political purges. This party, the HZDS (Movement for a Democratic Slovakia), led by Mečiar, was able to win broad populist support from across the spectrum and so achieved a central position in Slovakia. Political debate was about Czech/Slovak relations and the pace of political and economic reform, never about foreign policy or Gabčikovo, issues on which there was and is broad unity among Slovak parties, except the Hungarian parties. As the then Foreign Minister Jozef Moravčik put it, referring to differences of views between the political parties on foreign policy, "I do not see these differences as critical because both the government and the opposition share an equal desire to join the EC and NATO. We perhaps differ in some small procedural issues, but these do not seem crucial to me."[60]

The HZDS government party, led by Mečiar, won 74 out of the 150 seats in the Slovak national Council at the elections in 1992.[61] Initially, a coalition was formed with the Slovak National Party (SNS) with 14 seats, though its single SNS Minister soon resigned over divergences with Mr. Mečiar over economic reform. Eight HZDS deputies then formed a dissident faction. The opposition was composed of the Christian Democrats, led by Jan Čarnogursky with 17 seats (29 seats in 1990-1992) and the Democratic Left (SDL), led by Peter Weiss, with 32 seats, the second largest party. The SDL is at least in part the successor to the Communist Party. The Hungarian Minority Coalition, with Co-existence as its strongest component, won 14 seats. The Social Democratic Party, led by Alexander Dubček until his death in 1992, won no seats and has now entered an alliance with SDL. The Greens, which had held 6 seats in the 1990-1992 legislature, won no representation as interest in green issues seem, they hope merely temporarily, to be in decline.[62]

There is broad unity on the dam. For the HZDS, the Gabčikovo-Nagymaros project was a central plank in its 1992 election campaign. It was strongly defended and extolled by Vladimir Mečiar, as a fundamental Slovak achievement.[63] The issue was in the ministerial competence of Roman Hofbauer, a leading HZDS figure, close to Mečiar as a founder of the HZDS. The SNS also strongly supports the Gabčikovo-Nagymaros dam, regarding it as "a unifying symbol for all Slovaks."[64] The KDH, led by the Čarnogursky brothers, is also strongly supportive, even though KDH and Čarnogursky during his year as Premier was less nationalistic. The brother of the Party leader, Ivan Čarnogursky, is a Director of Hydrostav, a key water management company in Slovakia. Thus, the party programme states that it "will emphatically work for completing and implementing current (energy) projects as soon as possible. This concerns mainly the hydro-electric construction Gabčikovo and the Mochovce power plant."[65]

The SDL considers itself to be a pragmatic and non-ideological party of the left. It has taken a pragmatic and expert approach to the Gabčikovo-Nagymaros dam. It has supported both the original project and the Variant C.[66] Its Environmental Affairs Spokesman, Dr. Hrasko, was Deputy Chairman of the Environmental Committee of the Slovak National Council and Chairman of the Special Committee on Gabčikovo-Nagymaros. He became Environment Minister in the Moravčik coalition in 1994. The Social Democrats (SDS) consider that the issue should be depoliticised. For them, the Gabčikovo-Nagymaros project is a source of clean and cheap energy. The Party has supported the statements adopted by the Slovak National Council on the project.[67] Even the Greens, with some environmental conditions and a more watchful attitude than the other parties, nevertheless support the Gabčikovo-Nagymaros project.[68] Only the Hungarian parties are outright opponents, arguing that "two of the largest energy investments in Slovakia-- the Bös/Gabčikovo and Mohi/Mochovce atomic energy plant have a direct negative effect on the environment and endangers the ethnic structure of the Hungarian settlements."[69]

Hungary was much longer having its second post-communist election than Czecho-Slovakia/Slovakia. Perhaps due to the much more gradual reform process in Hungary, the first democratic election in 1990 was much less exclusively plebiscitary in character and more clearly laid the foundations for a stable party system than in Czechoslovakia. Indeed, the coalition established after the 1990 election lasted the full four-year term of the legislature, a unique event in central/eastern Europe. The party system itself changed far less than elsewhere during this first term. Even Prime Minister Antal, strong federator though he was, could not keep the lid on the factional in-fighting in his MDF, which was a very broad church, showing some of the same centrifugal tendencies as the more volatile Polish Solidarnosc or the Czech OF and Slovak VPN. By the time of his untimely death in December 1993 and his replacement by the more rightist Interior Minister, there had been both Nationalist/Populist splits, with the foundation of a new party by former MDF Vice-President Istvan Csurka, and liberal splits. At the same time, as in other post-communist political systems, the liberal opposition parties SDS and FIDESZ faced considerable difficulties in maintaining momentum, whereas the MSZP (ex-communists) showed signs of recovery and did, indeed, win the May 1994 elections with an absolute majority.

However, these internal political turbulences did not have much effect on the positions of the political parties in regard to the Gabčikovo-Nagymaros project. There was almost as broad unity, but this time against the project, as there is for it in Slovakia. However, many of the more committed critics of the Gabčikovo-Nagymaros project have regarded this unity as an unité de façade.[70] Probably, some Slovak political leaders have taken the same view, regarding Hungarian opposition as a temporary, historical phenomenon, maintained for electoralist reasons that would eventually disappear.[71] Thus, for example, few expected that it would be an important issue in the election of 1994 and nor was it.[72] Activists feared that the issue had been "used" by politicians and that public interest in it was waning, which might be a prelude to a sell-out on the issue. However, such nuances as there are in the positions of the Hungarian parties seem to relate only to criticisms of past and current tactics and to the degree of priority to be accorded to the question. Clearly, the new MZSP/SDS coalition is more ready to seek a compromise, but certainly not at any price.

In the 1990-94 Parliament, the three coalition parties--MDF, Christian Democrats (KDMP) and the Smallholders' Party--were singing more or less from the same song sheet. The MDF leadership and mainstream sought to remain in the cross-party consensus--against the Gabčikovo-Nagymaros project. It always sought a solution, but without ecological compromise. It underlined that the government had made compromise proposals, moving only gradually towards termination of the 1977 treaty. It had asked for EC mediation at an early stage and supported the Special Joint Parliamentary Committee, with the goal of improving relations between Hungary and Slovakia.[73] The National-Populist wing of the MDF regarded Hungary as stronger than Slovakia, which has less national legitimacy than Hungary and a worse European image, enabling Hungary to prevail over the Gabčikovo-Nagymaros project and the minorities related issues. The KDMP (Christian Democrats) was founded in 1989. Its environmental programme clearly stated the Party's opposition to the Gabčikovo-Nagymaros project. It regards the environmental situation as having deteriorated and sees no Slovak willingness to compromise on any acceptable basis, despite Hungarian proposals in that direction.[74] The Smallholders' Party was founded in 1988. It perhaps the most hardline of the former government parties. It insisted on raising the issue again in the election campaign, demanding demolition of Nagymaros. It has favoured a tough national consensus, developing contacts with the Hungarian minority and internationalisation of the issue, clearly rejecting the Slovak position on the division of the Danube waters.[75]

There were three parliamentary opposition parties in the 1990-1994 Parliament: the Free Democrats (SDS), FIDESZ (Young Democrats) and the Hungarian Socialist Party (MSZP). Outside Parliament there are groups of Green activists and within the Green movement, a very small minority supports the Gabčikovo-Nagymaros project. In general, those opposition parties emphasized the existence of broad unity with the former government and insist that this unified approach should be maintained. They criticized the MDF-led government for being rigid and inflexible, for having failed to anticipate Variant C and for not adequately internationalising the issue in good time before the Slovak fait accompli, which will be extremely difficult to reverse. They argued that a government formed by the opposition would work to advance a compromise, so as to improve the interim water management solution until the ICJ rules and mobilise international support for Hungary. The differences between the three then opposition parties were mainly nuances only. The Free Democrats (SDS)[76] emphasized the need to deal with the situation as it now is, with the reality of Variant C, and hence the need to find a compromise, but also to oblige Slovakia to respect its obligations under the 1992 London Protocol. To do so, it would build down the conflict and look for solutions that would meet Slovak legitimate demands, whilst building international support for the Hungarian position. FIDESZ's position is very similar to that of SDS: its criticism of the MDF government's weakness was the same. It would seek to depoliticise the issue, disassociate it from the issue of the Hungarian minority, and look for a double compromise with Slovakia and with the Hungarian ecologists in all parties.[77] For the MSZP, too, the problem is over-politicisation. It favours dialogue and compromise with Slovakia for a negotiated settlement, as pressure on Slovakia is, in its view, useless. It has thus favoured creative parliamentary and inter-party diplomacy.[78] The Greens, most active in the Györ area, are organised in NGOs such as REFLEX from Györ. They are active in a wide range of environmental issues and have developed international links such as with the WWF in Austria. Their main concern is vigilance: to hold the parties to a firm line. A very small group, the Realistic Green Club composed mainly of technocrats and scientists, seeks to reverse the dominance of the environmental extremists as they see it and to influence the political parties to reverse the cancellation of the Gabčikovo-Nagymaros project. It has sought close links with Slovakia. Its influence is extremely limited.

We have got well ahead of our narrative. Now we need to wind back to the position in early 1990 and follow the progress of the negotiations between Hungary and Czechoslovakia, having analysed the background that, as it were, set the boundaries of the margin of manoeuvre in each country.

Little serious happened in 1990. Positions hardened, as the new Hungarian government in its programme of May 22, 1990 stated that it "considered the construction of the Danube barrage system mistaken and will initiate as soon as possible negotiations on the rehabilitation and sharing of the damages with the Czechoslovak government to be elected."[79] Mr. Antall stated in Parliament that the programme would involve "preparations to stop the work on the Gabčikovo water works and to discuss the issue with the Czechoslovak Party. The Gabčikovo water works was born as a result of bad decisions and therefore we must bear in common the damages and consequences of putting it back into the original state."[80]

Clearly, this view was totally rejected by the Slovak side. There were fruitless exchanges of letters between Prime Ministers and Notes between governments throughout the year, with each side making its basic position clear, proposing talks, and exchanging technical and environmental studies. When direct discussions did finally occur on September 17-18, 1990, no significant progress was made, though the Czechoslovak side had up to that point desisted from any action to unilaterally divert the Danube and had taken action to study the environmental hazards involved in the project. This was not enough for Hungary.

It was now agreed to establish a joint inter-government commission, as proposed by the Czechoslovak Prime Minister in December 1990. However, the basis of discussion, from the Hungarian standpoint, remained renegotiation of the treaty to end the project, though as yet it had not begun to actually dismantle the work at Nagymaros, which was of course not yet very far advanced. Positions were hardening, though neither side had as yet acted irrevocably.

1991 saw a new round of fruitless negotiations,[81] attempts to internationalise the issue and a significant polarisation of positions that was ultimately to lead to unilateral termination of the treaty by the Hungarians and actual implementation of Variant C by the Slovaks. There were high level meetings, involving the senior plenipotentiaries of the two governments in Bratislava in January. The Slovak Prime Minister visited Budapest on February 8-9, 1991. The Hungarian-Czechoslovak Commission met in April 1991 with Minister without Portfolio Madl for Hungary and Prime Minister Mečiar for Slovakia. The Commission met again in June, and Czechoslovakia proposed involvement of the EC. However, given the resolution adopted by the Hungarian Parliament just before, on April 16, that called for negotiations "regarding the dissolution by joint action of the treaty signed on September 16, 1977" and for the "suspension of works on the territory of the Czech and Slovak Federated Republic," as well as "restoration and preservation of the region's ecological and natural values" and "rehabilitation of affected Hungarian territories," the Hungarian minister had no mandate to do other than negotiate cancellation. This meant a dialogue of the deaf. On July 15, the Commission met again (Čarnogursky-Madl), with the Czechoslovak side reiterating proposals to involve EC experts. This was repeated in September. Soon afterwards, the Slovak government (fifteen votes to six) decided to implement Variant C and on July 25, this decision was approved by the Federal Government, taking what was clearly the line of least resistance.[82]

In October, there were also joint discussions between the Environmental Committees of the two parliaments, but no significant progress was made. In December 1991, the Joint Commission held a third meeting, but no new ideas were on the table and no progress was made. The Czechoslovak side again proposed an expert Commission, including EC experts, but declined to stop work on Variant C, though it did agree that it would not be put into operation until at least the end of July 1992.

By now, Hungary was belatedly coming to realise that Variant C was a very real threat, which could only be met by combining a tough line with internationalising the dispute. Apart from an abortive Visegrad Foreign Ministers' discussion in January 1991, this tactic had up to then been resisted by Hungary. Thus, by letter of February 26, 1991, the Prime Minister accepted in principle the establishment of a trilateral commission, but set suspension of work on the provisional Variant C as a precondition. After preliminary contacts, Mr. Andriessen, Vice-President of the EC Commission, declared the Commission's readiness to take part in resolution of the dispute, but only by joint agreement and if both sides refrained from prejudicial action while the proposed trilateral commission sat. The Slovak side rejected these proposals as an ultimatum and set October 31 as the final date for implementation of Variant C. The trilateral commission could therefore not then be set up. After a final attempt to achieve agreement in the trilateral commission on May 6, 1992, the Hungarian government issued a declaration on May 19 by stating that it terminated unilaterally the 1977 treaty, associated protocols and agreements, as from May 23, 1992.[83] Parliament had authorised such a step if Czechoslovakia did not cease work on Variant C by April 30, 1992. This resolution belatedly now also called on the government to seek international support for its stand.[84] Hungary also at this point floated the idea of sending the issue to the International Court of Justice in the Hague. The Visegrad Summit, just before the June 1992 elections in Czechoslovakia, made no progress as the issue was too polarised. Hungary maintained its termination of the treaty and its proposal to go to the ICJ. Slovakia, by now in the driving seat, saw no reason to back down. By now, Variant C was well advanced and a halt to navigation on the Danube was officially announced to the Danube Commission on August 5, 1992.

Hungary now sought to belatedly internationalise the issue,[85] agreeing without conditions to the trilateral commission, reiterating its proposal to send the dispute to the ICJ, raising the issue in the CSCE and the Danube Commission. On October 14, Hungary called for a special session of the Danube Commission. On October 20, Prime Minister Antall appealed to world leaders to call for a stop to the implementation of Variant C. EC mediation broke down on October 22. There was a last-minute Slovak proposal to put the complete Dunakiliti dam into use. The significance of this was that Dunakiliti is in Hungarian territory. This would return the "key" to the division of Danube water to Hungary. This was not enough for Hungary. The Hungarians asked U.N. Secretary General Boutros-Ghali to intervene on October 24. The Danube Circle appealed to the Pope. The Hungarian

Government also sought to invoke a rarely used CSCE conflict prevention mechanism, but this was unavailing. In any event, Slovakia was determined to push Variant C through; as the end of October was the last feasible date in 1992 as later the waters would be too low.

The EC now began to be concerned about the real danger of serious conflict erupting between Slovakia and Hungary, and about possible impediments to navigation on the Danube, if Variant C was implemented without any external mediation. EC foreign ministers began to lean on both parties to avoid such a scenario.

Whilst on October 6, during a visit to Budapest, German Foreign Minister Klaus Kinkel said, he did not wish to take sides, he raised the subject at the Birmingham Special Council. Mandated by the EC, Kinkel took a strong line with the Czechoslovak Foreign Minister in Bonn on October 23, warning him that a unilateral diversion would strain relations. At the EC-Visegrad Summit in London on October 28, John Major led mediation efforts and exercising stronger pressure, brokered a tripartite (Hungary-Czechoslovakia-EC) agreement, called the London Protocol.[86] Under this protocol, it was agreed that all work on Variant C would be stopped at a date specified by the EC Commission on the basis of a tripartite fact-finding mission composed of one expert from each party. It also noted the commitment of the Czechoslovak side to maintain 95 percent of the Danube water in the old bed and to refrain from operating the power plant. It was also agreed to submit the dispute to binding international arbitration or to the International Court. This was a procedural agreement and was accepted on this basis only by Slovak Prime Minister Mečiar. Hungary has since complained that Slovakia has not met its commitment on the sharing of water between the old Danube and the new canal in Variant C. However, construction was suspended in November 1992, but the diversion remains, representing a major defeat for Hungary. In the spring of 1993, the parties reached agreement on a provisional water management regime and a joint submission of the dispute to the International Court of Justice, which we shall analyse in Chapter 7.

Notes

1. Dr. Liska, "The Aim of Safety and Benefits" in *Gabčikovo*, Bratislava: Vydala Narodna Obrada: 1993, p. 7.

2. For example, Julius Binder, *Damming Evidence: Gabčikovo, the Case for*, East European Reporter, September/October 1993, p. 77.

3. Figures from the Special Slovak Government brochure, *Gabčikovo*, MZR/SR, Bratislava, 1993, p. 3.

4. Figures from the booklet, *Man and Danube*, for the Exhibition on Gabčikovo-Nagymaros, held in the Slovak National Museum, Bratislava, Summer 1993.

5. Idem.

6. Interview in Budapest, September 9, 1993, with Dr. Jutlos, Chairman of the Club of (Hungarian) Real Greens.

7. *Results of an Expert Review Concerning the Ecological, Environmental, Technological, Economic, International and Legal Issues of the Bös-Nagymoros Barrage System, Budapest, Hardi Report*; September 1989, pp. 14-15, 16.

8. Hardi report, pp. 16-17.

9. Hardi report, p. 12.

10. Tamas Fleischer to the author, September 1993.

11. Hardi report, pp. 27-28.

12. *Energy in the Danubian Countries--Current Situation and Outlooks--Energy Proposals*, Report by the International Energy Council (1992).

13. Hardi report, p. 15.

14. B. Nagy, "The Danube Dispute: Conflicting Paradigms," in New Hungarian Review, Vol. XXXIII, No. 128, Winter 1992 (pp. 56-65), p. 56.

15. M.B. Liska, "Gabčikovo-Nagymaros: a Review of its Significance and its Impacts", Water Power and Dam Construction, July 1993, p. 37.

16. J. Binder, *Damming Evidence: Gabčikovo, the Case for*, East European Reporter, September/October 1992, p. 78.

17. Liska, "The Aim of Safety and Benefits," Water Power and Dam Construction, July 1993, p. 37.

18. Binder, *Damming Evidence: Gabčikovo, the Case for*, p. 78.

19. *Damming the Danube: What the Dam Builders Don't Want You to Know: a Critique of the Gabčikovo Dam Project*, SZOPK/SRN, Bratislava, 1993 for a debate on structural solidity, see section 9.

20. View expressed by Slovak Minister of Transport Roman Hofbauer.

21. J. Liptak, *The Danube of Europe*, Bratislava, NVK International: 1993, pp. 27-28.

22. Liptak, *The Danube of Europe*, p. 99.

23. Equipe Cousteau, *The Danube--For Whom, For What?*, Final Report, Paris 1993; traffic patterns, table 2.1 (p. 53); propositions for 2020, table 2.4 (p. 62).

24. Equipe Cousteau, *The Danube--For Whom, For What?*, pp. 63-66, for the analysis.

25. Equipe Cousteau, *The Danube--For Whom, For What?*, p. 176.

26. For a summary of the legal issues, see Nagy, "The Danube Dispute," pp. 58-64.

27. Political issues summarised in *Damming the Danube*, section 14 "Political Aspects of the Gabčikovo-Nagymaros Dam System."

28. T. Fleischer, "Jaws on the Danube: Water Management, Regime Change and the Movement Against the Middle Danube Hydro-electric Dam," International Journal of Urban and Regional Research, Vol. 17, No. 3 (1993), p. 44.

29. *Damming the Danube*, section R. "Political Aspects of the Gabčikovo-Nagymaros System."

30. Fleischer, "Jaws on the Danube," p. 432.

31. Janos Vargha, information provided to the author, interview in Budapest, September 8, 1993, in which he explained the background to his involvement with the issue.

32. Vargha, to the author, interview, September 8, 1993.

33. Vargha, to the author, interview, September 8, 1993.

34. Vargha, to the author, interview, September 8, 1993.

35. Fleischer, "Jaws on the Danube," pp. 433-434, on these shifting positions and this harder line.

36. On the origins of the Danube Circle, see A. Szekfü "Organisation, Spontaneity and Openness in the Danube Movements," presented to the Conference organised by the Hungarian Academy of Sciences on March 22, 1989. Also, information provided by Dr. Droppa, General Secretary of the Danube Circle, September 10, 1993.

37. Fleischer, "Jaws on the Danube," p. 433.

38. Interview with Pal Dragon, M.P. (Smallholders' Party) for Szentendre, September 9, 1993.

39. Fleischer, "Jaws on the Danube", 433-434.

40. Fleischer, "Jaws on the Danube," p. 435.

41. J. Vargha, to the author. He opposed this "politicisation."

42. Fleischer, "Jaws on the Danube," p. 436.

43. *Damming the Danube*, p. 3 quotes the Resolution in English.

44. Fleischer, "Jaws on the Danube," p. 436.

45. Sharon Fisher, "The Gabčikovo-Nagymaros Dam Controversy Continues," in International Relations, Vol. 2, No. 37, September 1993, RFE Report, p. 8.

46. Report by the Committee of Independent Specialists for the Council of Ministers, chaired by Professor Hardi, concerning the ecological, environmental, technological, economic, international and legal issues of the Bös-Nagymaros barrage system. Professor Peter Hardi was Director of the Hungarian Institute of International Affairs.

47. For a detailed, blow-by-blow chronology of events during this period, see *Damming the Danube*, pp. 3-6 and Ministry of Transport, Post and Telecommunications of the Slovak Republic, *The Gabčikovo Water Dam*, Bratislava, 1993, 9ff.

48. Quoted in the Declaration of the Government of the Hungarian Republic on the termination of the treaty concluded between the Peoples' Republic of Hungary and the Socialist Republic of Czechoslovakia on the construction and joint operation of the Gabčikovo-Nagymaros barrage system, signed in Budapest on September 16, 1977, dated May 19, 1992 (hereinafter "Hungarian Memorandum") which retraces the stages of the dispute, p. 7.

49. Cited in the Hungarian Memorandum, p. 8.

50. Hungarian Memorandum, paragraph 13, p. 8.

51. Nagy, "The Danube Dispute": "Projects should be stopped if there is "only" a higher probability, not certainty of damage," p. 57.

52. Fleischer, "Jaws on the Danube," p. 438.

53. *Damming the Danube*, section 12.

54. K. Okolicsanyi, "Slovak-Hungarian Tension: Bratislava diverts the Danube," International Relations (RFE Research Reports), vol. 1, No. 49, December 11, 1992, p. 49.

55. "Damming Evidence? Gabčikovo: the case for and the case against," contributed by Binder (for) and Vasarhelyi (against), East European Reporter, September-October 1992, p. 80.

56. For an excellent analysis of the split-up of Czechoslovakia and Havel's role in it, see K.-P. Schwarz, *Tschechen und Slowaken: Der Lange Weg zur Friedlichen Trennung*, Vienna-Zürich, Europa Verlag: 1993, pp. 210-228.

57. Quoted in Okolicsanyi, "Slovak-Hungarian Tension: Bratislava Diverts the Danube", p. 49.

58. Quoted in Okolicsanyi, "Slovak-Hungarian Tension: Bratislava Diverts the Danube", p. 50.

59. Schwarz, *Tschechen und Slowaken*, for an analysis of the Slovak political scene, pp. 212-218.

60. Interview in *Slovakia*, published by the News Agency of the Slovak Republic, Bratislava, 1993, p. 23.

61. Election results, in Schwarz, *Tschechen und Slowaken*, pp. 224-225.

62. Ms. Tothova, Deputy Chairperson, to the author, September 3, 1993.

63. Quoted in Okolicsanyi, "Slovak-Hungarian Tension: Bratislava Diverts the Danube," p. 50.

64. Mr. Prokeš, then SNS Deputy Speaker, to the author, interview, September 3, 1993.

65. The Election Manifesto of the Christian Democrat Movement of Slovakia (KDH), May 1992, p. 9.

66. Mr. Hrasko, to the author, interview, September 1, 1993.

67. SDS Vice-Chairman Dr. Bystricka, to the author, September 3, 1993.

68. Ms. Tothova, to the author, September 3, 1993.

69. *Hungarians in Slovakia*, Information Bulletin 9, Co-existence, Pozsony/Bratislava, 1992, p. 21.

70. For example, Mr. Droppa, Secretary-General of the Danube Circle, to the author, September 7, 1993.

71. Mr. Prokeš (SNS) for example told the author that he expected the Hungarians eventually to complete Nagymaros, interview, September 3, 1993.

72. Mr. Tatari, then State Secretary in the Hungarian Foreign Ministry, to the author, interview in Budapest, September 9, 1993.

73. Mr. Zebök, M.P. (MDF), to the author, Budapest, September 8, 1993.

74. Mr. Rott, M.P. (KDMP), Chairman of the Environment Committee, to the author, interview in Budapest, September 8, 1993.

75. Mr. Pal Dragon, M.P. (Smallholders' Party), interview, September 9, 1993.

76. Mr. Szent Ivanyi, M.P. (AFD), Spokesman for Foreign Affairs, interview, September 8, 1993.

77. Mr. Hegedüs, M.P. (FIDESZ), to the author, September 8, 1993.

78. Mr. Kovacs, M.P. (MSZD), Chairman of Foreign Affairs Committee, interview, September 8, 1993.

79. Declaration of the Government of the Hungarian Republic, May 22, 1990, p. 10.

80. Cited in, Ministry of Transport, Post and Telecommunications and Public Works of the Slovak Republic, *The Gabčikovo Water Dam*, p. 14.

81. Chronicle of negotiations, ibid., pp. 14-28.

82. B. Nagy, "A Hungarian Chronology of the Bös (Gabčikovo/Nagymaros dam system," p. 60.

83. Declaration of the Government of the Republic of Hungary on the termination of the Treaty, signed in Budapest on September 17, 1977, dated May 19, 1992.

84. Resolution of March 24, 1992 regarding the inter-state treaty of 1977 concluded between the Peoples' Republic of Hungary and the Czechoslovak Socialist Republic regarding the construction and operation of the Bös-Nagymaros barrage system.

85. See Okolicsanyi, "Slovak-Hungarian Tension: Bratislava Diverts the Danube," pp. 51-53.

86. Agreed minutes of the meeting between the European Commission, the CSFR and Hungary on October 28, 1992, on the Gabčikovo-Nagymaros project.

7

The Legal Issues
and International Mediation

From mid-1991, the idea of a third party mediation in the dispute by the EC Commission was floated, and in October 1992 was finally accepted by both parties in October 1992 as a stepping stone towards referring the case to the International Court of Justice in The Hague. The case was sent to the ICJ by the special agreement of April 7, 1993. How and why did the EC Commission become involved in the dispute?

From a very early stage, the Hungarians raised the idea of involving foreign ecological experts in the issue and formally suggested this to the Czechoslovak government on January 12, 1990. Basically, they wanted international legitimisation of their environmental case. In October 1990, the Czechoslovak government made a counter-proposal: a joint approach to the EC for a PHARE programme project on the ecology of the region. As we have seen, the negotiations between the parties made no headway. Indeed, through 1991 the dispute escalated, with threats to terminate the 1977 treaty from the Hungarian side and to implement Variant C from the Slovak side.

The European Community in the meanwhile was redefining its relationship with the whole central European region. It recognised the dramatic and indeed historic nature of the events of 1989-1990 and the need to respond. However, these developments were then perceived as not only an opportunity that might not also easily recur, but also a danger, in two senses. The need to respond could divert the EC from its own internal integration and the Community might be confronted by instability on its borders if developments in the region turned sour.

The Community was searching for a balanced response that met all these contradictory needs. To that end, it held two special European Councils Strasbourg on December 8-9, 1989 and Dublin on April 28, 1990). Whilst early membership, desired by many in the region, was not considered a realistic or desirable option by the EC, a more coherent approach, going beyond the "first generation" trade and cooperation agreements and aid programmes, was clearly required. As Mr. Andriessen, then EC Commissioner for External Affairs put it as early as June 1990, "The European Community is willing to accept its co-responsibility for what is going on in those countries."[1] By the time of the Lisbon European Council in June 1992, the Community had reached a new consensus that the EFTA enlargement could proceed without institutional "deepening" and that the new generation of Europe Agreements with at least the three (later four) leading Central European states (Poland, Hungary and Czechoslovakia) should represent a clear pre-accession phase for these countries, though of indeterminate length. This approach was confirmed in the Edinburgh and Copenhagen European Councils in December 1992 and June 1993. It stressed the political, as well as the economic content of the European Agreements. For the first time, the Copenhagen European Council also held out the possibility of membership. Hungary (as did Poland) applied formally in April 1994.

The strong desire of the central European states to become full members of the EC as rapidly as possible gives the EC (now EU) considerable political leverage in the region. Despite the decision of principle taken in Copenhagen, the EC itself will still determine the pace of integration.

The EC wanted to establish a gradualist rapprochement based on intensification of the political dialogue between the EU and the central European associated states. This would eventually involve including the Visegrad states in a "political area" in advance of full membership.[2] The EU also wants to encourage regional cooperation, such as the Visegrad Group, the central European free trade area and the central Caribbean initiative as part of the preparation of the central European states for full membership. Regional cooperation is also seen as a forum for solving regional problems *before* full membership. Both the Visegrad-EC Declaration in Luxembourg and the Summit in London on October 1992 were part of this process.[3] Clearly, the Hungarians and Slovaks were on notice to act in a cooperative and responsible manner, acceptable to the EC.

Clearly, this would be undermined if there was a serious conflict between some of the parties, that could extend into other areas, such as the problem of the Hungarian minority in Slovakia, and threaten stability in the Region. The EC had not only the incentive but also an urgent need to intervene to dampen down the ongoing conflict over the dam in 1991/92. Clearly too, the EC had some powerful sticks and carrots, such as PHARE, trade relations and its control of the pace of development in political relations which could give bite to its good offices. The EC though, had been reluctant to become too deeply involved, fearing the risk of failure, or the ultimate need to take sides in the dispute. It therefore clearly stated that it could only become involved if there was a joint consensual approach from both parties and would only set itself the limited goal of defusing the issue by getting agreement for the case to go to the International Court in the Hague by special agreement between the parties.[4]

Initially, the Hungarians were the most eager to achieve EC political involvement and they raised this at the political level, after refusing to respond to several earlier Czechoslovak proposals to include EC environmental experts in a low-key trilateral expert commission.[5] Hungarian Minister Madl made an approach to Mr. Andriessen on March 18, 1992. Mr. Andriessen's response was his letter of April 13, 1992 to the two Foreign Ministers announcing willingness to play a mediating role but also setting out the limits of such a mission. Proposals for a first meeting in Vienna in May 1992 failed, as the Hungarian side did not attend. By late summer 1992, both sides were talking of going to the International Court of Justice (ICJ) whilst continuing on their unilateral paths and a possible agreement on a joint approach to the EC began to emerge. On October 28, 1992, the EC and the parties agreed a Protocol[6] in London. This involved agreements to stop work on Variant C, to negotiate a provisional water management scheme (in which the EC would remain involved) and to refer the dispute to the International Court. Accordingly, a special agreement to send the dispute to the Court was reached on April 7, 1993[7] and sent to the Court on July 2, 1993.

How will the ICJ handle the case? The International Court of Justice was created by the United Nations Charter in 1945, though it succeeded two earlier international courts and in particular the Permanent Court of International Justice established as part of the League of Nations machinery.[8] Article 7 of the U.N. Charter includes the ICJ among the organs of the U.N. Articles 92-96 of the Charter deal with the organisation and role of the ICJ, declaring it to be "the principal judicial organ of the United Nations."[9] Article 94 lays down that Member States shall comply with rulings of the ICJ in cases to which they are party and that the Security Council may be called upon to take measures to enforce rulings. The Security Council may also recommend that states refer matters in dispute to the ICJ.[10]

The Court was, during the Cold War and decolonisation period, in the words of Secretary-General Boutros-Ghali in his report "An Agenda for Peace," "an under-used resource."[11] Court President Sir Robert Jennings was able to note a significant increase in the role of the Court in his 1991 address to the General Assembly. He called for the Court to be used even more often and more effectively, as a tool of preventative diplomacy, in tandem with other U.N. instruments.[12] Speaking to the Rio Conference, the ICJ Registrar argued that the Court could play an important role in developing and enforcing environmental international law, going beyond the important principles already established, for example in the 1948 Cornu Channel case, where the Court ruled that states could not knowingly allow the use of their territory in such a way as to harm other states.[13] These two new concerns are both relevant to the Gabčikovo-Nagymaros case where, as we have seen, the European Union sought to use reference to the ICJ as a means of defusing the dispute and where issues of environmental damage will be central to the case.

Under the Statute of the Court,[14] its jurisdiction can be established in several different ways. States may declare--in advance and in general--that they will accept the jurisdiction of the ICJ. That acceptance may be unqualified, save for a condition of reciprocity. On the other hand, it may contain minor reservations, only such as exclusion of matters where other disputes procedures have been agreed, or it may contain wide-ranging exclusions. The declaration may be limited or unlimited in duration. In any case, it is revocable. To date, 55 states have made such a declaration, including Poland, Bulgaria and Estonia, but neither Hungary nor Czechoslovakia had done so at the relevant time.

Article 36(1) of the ICJ Statute provides for an alternative and more ad hoc jurisdiction based on a special agreement between the parties to refer a matter to the court. The special agreement signifies agreement to accept jurisdiction, determines the issues on which the Court is asked to rule and may establish some special ancillary or procedural provisions. Hungary and Slovakia concluded a special agreement on April 7, 1993 in Brussels and jointly so notified the Court on July 2, 1993.

International treaties (nearly 300 in all) can contain compromissary clauses that establish jurisdiction for the ICJ--clearly not the case in the 1977 Gabčikovo-Nagymaros treaty. Under Article 96 of the U.N. Charter, the U.N. organs and authorised U.N. specialised agencies can ask the Court to give an advisory opinion on an issue of international law.

To date, the Court has given 56 judgements and 21 advisory opinions. At present, nine cases and one advisory opinion are pending.[15]

The Court has fifteen judges. They are elected by the U.N. Security Council and General Assembly for a term of nine years, renewable. One-third are renewed every three years to maintain continuity. The judges elect their President and Vice-President. The Statute only specifies that the main civilisations and legal traditions of the world should be represented, but a custom of regional representation has grown up. There are normally judges from the five permanent members of the Security Council, two others from western Europe, one from eastern Europe, two from Latin America, two from Asia, two from Africa and one from the Middle East. There is now a Hungarian judge. The Statute provides that in a case where there is not a judge of the nationality of one or both parties, they may appoint judges ad hoc, raising the size of the Court to sixteen or seventeen. In the Gabčikovo-Nagymaros case, Slovakia may thus appoint an ad hoc judge, who will not necessarily be a Slovak. The Court takes its decisions by majority votes and concurring and dissenting opinions are published. The ICJ works in only two official languages--English and French.

When a case is filed, the parties first enter a written phase, usually involving exchange in according with a timetable laid down by the Court, of a memorial from the plaintiff, a counter-memorial from the defendant and possibly a reply and a rejoinder. Special agreements can modify these arrangements. This phase may typically take up to two years. Thereafter, two rounds of oral hearings are held. Here, witness and experts may be heard and the judges can and indeed often do ask questions of the parties on issues of both fact and law.

The deliberation, prior to judgement, is governed by internal rules laid down in 1976.[16] The President, after a debate in the Court, establishes the questions to be addressed. Judges are then given a time limit to submit papers addressing those issues and suggesting a tentative disposal of the case. From these, an indication of where the majority lies will emerge. A drafting committee of the President (if he is in the majority) or another senior judge, as chairman and two judges from the majority, is elected. It proposes a draft which goes through two readings with written amendments and then a formal vote is taken in the full court on the final text of the judgement. The judgement is read in open court and published with dissenting and concurring opinions appended to it.

In the Gabčikovo-Nagymaros case, the special agreement[17] has in effect submitted two cases or cross claims. Accordingly, there is no plaintiff/defendant situation as such. Article 2 of the special agreement submits three questions to the Court:

1.   whether Hungary was permitted to suspend work on Gabčikovo-Nagymaros unilaterally in 1989,
2.   the legality of Variant C,

3.   the legality of the termination of the treaty of 1977 by Hungary in 1992.

Points 1 and 3 are complaints against Hungary and 2 is a complaint against Slovakia. The issues have been deliberately submitted as a package. The Court is asked to consider the issues on the basis of the 1977 treaty, other relevant treaty law and, importantly, general principles of international law. The Court is asked to determine "the legal consequences, including the rights and obligations for the parties arising from its judgement." In Article 4, the parties agree to establish a temporary water management regime with the involvement of outside experts from the EC and if necessary with their mediation, but they foreswear having recourse to a request for provisional measures under Article 41 of the Statute of the ICJ. This point, no doubt of key importance to Slovakia, is declared as "fundamental to the conclusion and validity of the special agreement" (Article 4(3)). Under Article 5, the parties commit themselves to accept and execute the ICJ's judgement (in fact, no more than their Charter obligations) and to enter into immediate negotiations to that end with the possibility of a further appeal to the Court after six months as to modalities of executing the initial judgement.

On the procedure, it was agreed (Article 3) that there should be a parallel exchange of memorials and counter-memorials and possible parallel replies. The Court set May 5, 1994 as the deadline for memorials and December 5, 1994 as the deadline for counter-memorials which have been met by both parties. There was a possibility of tabling Reply Memorials by June 20, 1995. Both sides made use of this supplementary reply possibility in order to address key issues of fact and law in relation to the environmental impact of the project and problems of chronology in regard to threats to terminate the treaty and to implement Variant C. Oral arguments are due in 1996, and it is likely that judgement will not be given until late in that year. This would mean about two and a half to three years elapsing between filing and judgement. It is not a fast track, but nor is it excessively slow.

The Court shall (Article 38 of the ICJ Statutes) take account of international treaties binding the parties, international custom, and in addition general principles of international law and judicial decisions and legal literature as subsidiary sources of rules of international law. Indeed, in the Gabčikovo-Nagymaros case, both parties will be relying in some degree on general principles of international law as well as on the treaty. In fact, the Slovak party bases its case on non-performance of the 1977 treaty by the Hungarian party and in relation to Variant C on its right to take measures in line with the aims of the treaty without the agreement of the defaulting

Hungarian party. The Hungarian party relies on general principles of international law to release it from the 1977 treaty. Clearly, the Court would have to weigh the various sources of international law and practice and apply them to this case and might indeed come to a balanced conclusion, condemning both parties partially. Indeed, the submission of the issues as a package almost invites the Court to consider this approach.

Enforcement of judgements of the ICJ is a major issue because the Court itself has no means of coercion against a party that fails to respect the judgement of the ICJ. The U.N. Charter, unlike the Statute of the International Court of Arbitration, does not empower states to act by military or other coercive means to enforce the judgement in its favour. Only the U.N. Security council is empowered to act to enforce the judgements of the Court.

What are the legal positions of the parties in this case? The memorials of the two sides, tabled by May 5, 1994 and the counter-memorials are under court rules, still confidential. Their general tenour is known to the author. What follows is based on previously published sources, but is known to be in line with the arguments in the memorials. The key issues for determination will be the interpretation and application to this case of the general rules of international law on unilateral termination of treaties, the legal value of international environmental commitments undertaken after the 1977 treaty (so-called soft law), the role of COMECON in relation to Hungary's changed circumstances defence and the chronology of various Slovak and Hungarian unilateral actions.[18]

The Slovakian position is the more straightforward and simple. They argue that the 1977 treaty and the later amending protocols remain fully valid. The later Hungarian suspensions and actions are, in the Slovak view, unilateral and illegal.[19] The measures taken by Hungary to dismantle parts of the Gabčikovo-Nagymaros works on Hungarian territory and restore the area are also regarded by Slovakia as illegal. Under Article 8(1) of the 1977 treaty, these works are the joint property of the two parties. Therefore, the Hungarian party is *not* entitled to dispose of them unilaterally. The fact that the complex negotiations between the parties failed, despite what the Slovaks consider as willingness to compromise, did not, in the Slovak view, authorise the Hungarian state to terminate the treaty unilaterally. In the Slovak view, the treaty could only be terminated or amended by mutual agreement and consent. Slovakia has insisted on fulfilment of a treaty "concluded and duly signed on September 16, 1977. Should the international community give its recognition to the actions taken so far by the Hungarian side, this would create a precedent for unilateral termination of any international treaty."[20] Clearly, this point will be serious food for thought for the Court.

The Slovak side regards Variant C not as a riposte, but as a responsible and inevitable reaction to non-fulfilment by the Hungarian side: "This solution was chosen as a consequence of unilateral withdrawal from the treaty and the Czechoslovak side only resorted to it after all other possibilities of reaching an agreement on a common course of action had been exhausted."[21] Slovakia argues that it was justified in acting to defend its interests, and that it has done so in a manner that remains on Slovak territory and has not dangerously affected the environment and in particular the ground water in Hungary. It argues that Variant C was deliberately chosen precisely so as to remain within the goals of the contract of 1977. Slovakia sought, as it were without the Hungarian party, to nevertheless implement the aims of the 1977 treaty, which in its eyes remained valid.

The Hungarian case is more complex and more difficult to make. The Hungarian side argues that it made repeated and persistent efforts to reach agreement with the Czechoslovak party after it had become convinced by expert opinion that the project posed serious environmental risks to both sides, but met with a blank refusal to suspend or cancel the treaty on every occasion, with the Czechoslovak side "regarding those (expert) opinions as unfounded."[22] The Hungarian memorandum signifying termination makes those arguments as a preface to the statement that the Hungarian party had decided to terminate the treaty. This implies that Hungary had no option or was virtually compelled to terminate the treaty as an act of environmental self-defence, justified by reference to the general norms of international law.

Yet, the 1977 treaty makes no provision for termination and so normally it can only be terminated by the consent of the parties. International law places much weight on the presumption of respect for international treaties enshrined in the maxim "pacta sunt servanda." Traditionally, international law recognises only very narrow grounds for unilateral termination of a treaty obligation. These have been codified in the 1969 Vienna Convention, which has only been in force between the parties since 1987 and hence cannot directly be applied to this case. Yet, in the Iceland Fisheries case, the ICJ stated that the Vienna Convention could be considered as a codification of the generally recognised principles of international law in regard to treaties. The Vienna Convention lays down three basic limited conditions for unilateral termination of a treaty. The first condition is impossibility of a fulfilment. This claim could clearly not be made by Hungary. The more relevant conditions relate to a "material breach of a bilateral treaty"[23] or a fundamental change in circumstances. The breach of the treaty must be a "material" one of some importance. The "fundamental change of circumstances" must be a change that could not have been foreseen by the parties at the time of conclusion of the treaty. Furthermore, the circumstances subsequently altered, must have constituted "an essential basis of the consent of the parties to be bound by the treaty."[24] The mere fact that opinions of the treaty have changed and that most Hungarians now consider the treaty a bad commitment cannot justify termination if the other party insists on performance.[25]

The Hungarian side argues that the failure of the Czechoslovak party to undertake environmental works, in particular water purifying plants, constitute a breach of Articles 15 and 19 of the 1977 treaty requiring the parties to "ensure that the quality of water in the Danube is not impaired by the construction and operation of the system of locks" (paragraph 15(1)) and "ensure compliance with the obligations for the protection of nature arising in connection with the construction and operation of the system of locks" (paragraph 19). These failures represent, in the Hungarian view, a "material breach of a bilateral treaty" and hence in the words of the Vienna Convention, "a ground for terminating the treaty."[26] Yet is this breach, if established, sufficiently important to warrant the extreme remedy of unilateral termination?

Second, Hungary invokes the rebus sic stantibus ground of a fundamental change in circumstances, also derived from the Vienna Convention. This is not merely a general argument that there has been a regime change. Such an argument would, ironically, too closely resemble the old Soviet doctrine of unequal treaties. The Hungarian argument stands on the second of only two preambular statements in the 1977 treaty. The first preamble is economic in content. The second is political. It refers to the treaty project as serving to "significantly contribute to bringing about the socialist integration of the State Members of the Council for Mutual Economic Assistance"(COMECON). This is the only political grounding of the treaty and appears on an apparently equal footing with the economic preamble. Clearly, "socialist integration" and COMECON have disappeared as goals of both economies and societies which, since 1989, are moving in a quite different direction. Hungary regards the COMECON interest in the project as a central element in the original plan as its disappearance as a fundamental change. However, this issue will have to be more closely addressed in the course of the ICJ proceedings. Slovakia rejects this view, emphasizing a classic view of continuity of state obligations. It regards the question of political change as irrelevant, but has rarely addressed the specific question of COMECON integration raised by Hungary.[27] This will clearly be an important issue for the Court.

Third, Hungary invokes violation of general rules of international environmental law by Slovakia. These general rules of international law on environmental protection have developed since the signature of the 1977 treaty. Hungary argues that these take precedence over earlier treaty provisions.

Several such provisions are cited such as principle 4 of the Stockholm Declaration which prescribes that "nature preservation including wildlife must therefore receive importance in the planning of economic development." Principle 3 of the 1982 General Assembly World Charter for Nature states that "special protection shall be given to unique areas, to be representative samples of all different types of ecosystems and to the habitats of rare or endangered species."[28] The Slovak side would argue that these provisions are not legally binding and in any case are too general as to preclude the Gabčikovo-Nagymaros dam system.[29]

Hungary has also argued that the "construction and operation of the dam causes an ecological necessity which precludes the wrongfulness of termination."[30] A grave and eminent peril has been created by the dam project, contends Hungary. This, it argues, is a norm of international law that appears in Article 33(1) of the Draft of the United Nations International Commission on State Responsibility. A state can, as laid down in this draft, invoke a state of necessity if "an act was the only means of safeguarding an essential interest of the state against a grave and imminent peril." The Slovaks would argue that such as yet non-binding commitments do not override treaty obligations. One difficult problem for Hungary is the fact that by the time of the 1989 Protocol that confirmed and indeed accelerated the project, the environmental considerations that perhaps were not known in 1977, were fully known by then. However, will the Court in any case regard this as hard, binding law?

The second issue that the International Court of Justice will have to resolve will be the legality under international law of the implementation of Variant C. As we have seen, Slovakia argues that it was virtually obliged to implement Variant C in the face of Hungarian refusals to compromise on the basis of a 1991 parliamentary resolution that bound the Hungarian government to cancellation and returning the site. Some argue that this deprived the Hungarian government of negotiating flexibility and provoked the Slovaks into deciding on Variant C. Indeed, some would go as far as to say that the decision on Variant C was, initially at least, a bluff, never intended to be carried out, aimed at pressuring Hungary to return to the original joint project. Slovakia now argues that Variant C is a legal action insofar as it does no more than carry out the intention of the 1977 treaty and its provisions, as far as that is still possible.[31]

In the Hungarian view,[32] Variant C is an illegal act because the diversion of the Danube out of the old bed violates Hungarian sovereignty and territorial integrity and violates the character of the international border to Hungary's detriment. It is also argued that the diversion of the Danube violates "the rule of customary international law regulating the status and usage of cross-boundary environmental resources such as international rivers."[33] The Hungarians note that the Danube is in the relevant section on international border. It is under the jurisdiction of both states and subject to several treaties such as the 1978 bilateral treaty on water management of boundary rivers that stipulates joint management of such waters. The provisional solution--Variant C--violates customary rules of international environmental law, argues the Hungarian side referring to various U.N. Declarations and draft conventions of the United Nations Law Commission, in particular its draft on the law of non-navigational uses of water courses. Here, clearly the Slovak side, does not accept that these texts are binding between the parties or that they supersede the terms of the 1977 treaty. The Hungarian side also argues that the provisional solution is in contradiction to the spirit of the Danube Convention of 1948. Certainly, the Danube Convention does not specifically deal with the case of a unilateral diversion of the river, but in general terms, it lays down that all works carried out due to unforeseen circumstances should be carried out only with the prior consent of all the riparian states, and that has clearly not been obtained in this case.[34]

However, the most serious contention of the Hungarian side against the legality of the provisional Variant C in terms of international law lies in the issue of the Danube as the border between the two countries.[35] The Slovak side argues that the actual border itself has not been moved north by the diversion of the river into Slovak territory, and hence there has been no violation of the treaties establishing the border between the two countries.[36] Clearly, this is literally true. In the Hungarian view, the character of the border has been radically altered and of course with it, the rights for example over navigation in that section of the river, as the residual old Danube channel can support no serious navigation. The main *navigation* channel is however designated as the border by Article 27(4) of the treaty of Trianon of 1920, confirmed by paragraph 1(4a) of the treaty of Paris (1947) and finally by the bilateral treaty concerning the Regime of State Frontiers concluded in 1956 in its Article 2(3). The 1976 treaty on water management also seems to exclude unilateral measures. The diversion of the main navigation channel, leaving only 20 percent of the water in the old channel, thus alters the character of the border in a significant manner because "the main course of navigation no longer correlates with the borderline, depriving Hungary of its lawful jurisdiction over a major economic lifeline."[37] Furthermore, under a fundamental rule of international law, long established by the ICJ and earlier International Arbitration decisions, states may not cause harm to other riparian states from their territory.[38]

Clearly, the ICJ will have to unravel a complex web of claims and counter-claims that are in themselves interrelated. Would the illegality of the Hungarian termination of the 1977 treaty by unilateral decision in any sense make the implementation of Variant C legal, if it were not otherwise? Would the threat of implementation of Variant C--if that were an illegal action- make the unilateral termination of the treaty legal if it were otherwise not? In any event, the special agreement binds together the three issues: the Hungarian suspension of work in 1989, the termination of the treaty in 1992 and Variant C.

Some argue that the Court should and perhaps will seek an elegantly balanced ruling that find both the unilateral termination of the treaty and Variant C illegal actions under international law. The bottom line arguments on unilateral termination relate to the strength and exceptions to the cornerstone principle of pacta sunt servanda that should be permitted. The Court must decide if the change of circumstances that intervened there are so strong but also so unique and localised as not to constitute too broad a precedent that others would seek to misappropriate. Only then could the Court reasonably accept the Hungarian view. The Court has only on one obvious occasion considered such arguments of "changed circumstances" as grounds for release from a treaty obligation. That was in the Iceland Fisheries case in 1974.[39] Here in its ruling, the Court adopted the narrowest basis for judgement and avoided general analysis of the rebus sic stantibus doctrine. It appeared to say then that it could only accept a narrow application of this doctrine.

In the Gabčikovo-Nagymaros case, it will be more difficult to avoid this key question which is at the heart of the case. The Court may not wish to adopt a broad interpretation, of rebus sic stantibus, so as not to create usable precedents for others. In that case, the treaty would stand, unless Hungary's other weaker arguments are persuasive. In relation to Variant C, the bottom line issue here is the change in character of the Trianon border and the concomitant violation of Hungarian rights. The argument is that a unilateral action that otherwise clearly appears to violate some basic principles of international law can be justified if they would implement the goals of the litigious treaty. But, a treaty is not just the ends, but also the means. If the Slovak view is that the treaty stands, it would be paradoxical for the Slovak party to itself violate the treaty, at least as to the means, if not as to the ends. The Court might find this a difficult and risky construction. This could lead it to find that both the unilateral termination and Variant C were legally unjustified. Taken literally, this would oblige Slovakia to abandon Variant C and Hungary to open Dunakiliti and finish Gabčikovo-Nagymaros. Neither party would wish to take these particular actions at this point and so would be obliged to compromise on a jointly agreed solution, within the parameters of the Court ruling.

The European Union would undoubtedly be in a position to exercise leverage to induce compliance with the final judgement of the ICJ, not least because both states are applying for EU membership. The main concern of the EU will be stability in the region. As indicated, non- compliance can be considered by the Security Council, which may recommend measures to bring about compliance, but pressure by the European Union is more likely to effective. This would be reinforced if in line with several European Parliament resolutions, the EU were to consider financial support for either or both states to cover losses of earnings from electricity generation or for financial measures to return the area around the dam to its natural state,[40] as part of a compromise settlement implementing the ICJ's ruling.

As we have seen throughout this book, the dam project is highly symbolic and potentially an explosive threat to the stability of the region. For the moment, referral of the issue to the International Court and the mediation efforts of the European Union, which contributed to achieving that result, have cooled the dispute down and put it on the back-burner. This is exemplary for what is needed in terms of crisis management in the region. This external concern has also contributed to bringing about an improvement in relations between Slovakia and Hungary, as more cooperative governments have taken office in the two countries. However, the dispute could always take off again, and the judgements of the ICJ will be a potential flash point. For the moment, the dispute is evolving positively, but continued vigilance is still required to ensure that this positive evolution does continue.

Notes

1. Speech by Mr. Frans Andriessen, "Europe at the Crossroads: the EC in a Changing Political and Economic Environment", Brussels, June 8, 1990.

2. Mr. Michael Leigh, Member of the Cabinet of Vice-President Andriessen at the relevant time, to the author, February 1994.

3. On the strategy of the EC and the Visegrad Group and the Central European Initiative, see J. Fitzmaurice, "Regional Cooperation in Central Europe" in West Europe on Politics, Vol. 16, No. 3, July 1993 (pp. 380-400), especially pp. 391-397.

4. Michael Leigh to the author, February 1994.

5. Chronology in *The Waterworks Dam Gabčikovo*, published by the Ministry of Transport, Telecommunications and Public Works of the Slovak Republic, November 1992, pp. 18-24.

6. Agreed Minutes of the Meeting between the European Commission, the CSFR and Hungary on October 28, 1992 on the Gabčikovo-Nagymaros project.

7. Special Agreement, signed in Brussels.

8. On the Court, see S. Rosenne, *The Law and Practise of the International Court*, (2 vols.), Leiden, 1965.

9. U.N. Charter, Article 92.

10. U.N. Charter, Article 36(3).

11. *An Agenda for Peace - Preventative Diplomacy, Peace-Making and Peace-Keeping*, cited in ICJ Year Book 1991/92 (No. 46) at pp. 218-219.

12. Sir Robert Jennings, Address to the 44th Meeting of the 46th Session of the General Assembly, November 8, 1991, ICJ Year Book 1991/92, pp. 207-210.

13. Registrar Valencia Ospina speaking to the Rio Conference (June 3-14, 1992), cited in ICJ Year Book 1991/92, pp. 212-218.

14. The Statute and Rules of the Court on which the following was drawn, published in ICJ *Acts and Documents Concerning the Organisation of the Court* (No. 5), 1989. Statute at pp. 60-89 and rules at pp. 92-161 (hereafter Acts and Documents).

15. Data as of March 1994, supplied by the Court's press office.

16. Published in Acts and Documents, resolution concerning the internal practice of the Court (April 12, 1976), pp. 165-173.

17. *Special Agreement Between the Republic of Hungary and the Slovak Republic for Submission to the International Court of Justice of the Differences Between Them Concerning the Gabčikovo-Nagymaros Project*, jointly notified on July 2, 1993.

18. *Declaration of the Government of the Republic of Hungary on Termination of the Treaty Concluded Between the Peoples' Republic of Hungary and the Socialist Republic of Czechoslovakia on Construction and Joint Operation of the Gabčikovo-Nagymaros Barrage System, signed in Budapest on September 16, 1967*, Budapest, May 1992, pp. 1-2 (Hungarian Declaration).

19. For example, *Declaration of the National Council of the Slovak Republic About the Gabčikovo-Nagymaros Dam Project*, adopted on March 24, 1993, part 1 (Slovak Declaration).

20. Slovak Declaration, part 1.

21. Slovak Declaration, point 3.

22. *Bös-Nagymaros File*, published by Ferenc Madl, Hungarian Minister without Portfolio, October 1992, p. 7.

23. Cited and analysed in Nagy, op. cit., p. 59 and L. Caflisch, "Unequal Treaties" in German Year Book of International Law, Vol. 35 (1992), pp. 52-80, especially pp. 78-80 on the "changed circumstances" issue.

24. Article 62(1) of the Vienna Convention, 1969, cited and analysed in Nagy, op. "The Danube Dispute", pp. 59-60.

25. B. Nagy, "The Danube Dispute: Conflicting Paradigms," The New Hungarian Quarterly, Vol. XXXIII, No. 128, Winter 1992, p. 59.

26. See Hungarian Declaration, part 4, pp. 25-26 for statements quoted and analysis of this issue.

27. Hungarian Declaration, pp. 24-25.

28. Nagy, "The Danube Dispute," p. 60 for citation.

29. Nagy, "The Danube Dispute," pp. 60-61 examines this issue.

30. Declaration 23.

31. Views expressed by Minister Hofbauer to the author, September 4, 1993.

32. Hungarian Declaration, p. 5(o) and 5(b), p. 26.

33. *Bös-Nagymaros File*, p. 15.

34. Hungarian Declaration, p. 5(f).

35. Hungarian Declaration, p. 5(b) and Nagy, "The Danube Dispute," pp. 61-62.

36. Slovak Declaration, point 4.

37. Nagy, "The Danube Dispute", p. 62.

38. Nagy, "The Danube Dispute," p. 63.

39. Fisheries Jurisdiction (U.K. v. Iceland) Merits Judgement of July 25, 1974, International Court of Justice Reports, 1974, p. 3.

40. Views expressed to the author by Mr. Tatari, State Secretary in the Hungarian Ministry of Foreign Affairs, interview in Budapest, September 1993.

About the Book and Author

The conflict between Hungary and Slovakia over the Gabčikovo-Nagymaros dam system on the Danube is a potentially explosive threat to regional stability along this key economic artery between the North Sea and the Black Sea. Emblematic of the difficulties in establishing a post-communist regional order, this bitter battle between material economic values and post-materialist environmental and cultural values threatens to resurrect nationalist resentments buried by forty years of communism.

Based on a wealth of primary research, this balanced book considers the broad political, economic, social, legal, and environmental implications of the dam project—not just for Hungary and Slovakia, but for Europe as a whole. Viewing the controversy from the contending perspectives of all the key players, the author explores the role of outside mediation efforts and the resulting implications for regional security and cooperation.

John Fitzmaurice is professor at the Institute of European Studies of the University of Brussels and is administrator in the General Secretariat of the Commission of the European Communities in the Department for Liaison with the European Parliament.

Index